THE ART OF
BREATHING

THE ART OF
BREATHING

Nancy Zi

BANTAM BOOKS
TORONTO · NEW YORK · LONDON · SYDNEY · AUCKLAND

THE ART OF BREATHING

A Bantam Book / June 1986

Designed and produced by the Compage Company, San Francisco, California.

Illustrations by Eric Maché.
Book design by Joy Dickinson.

New Age and the accompanying figure design as well as the statement "a search for meaning, growth and change" are trademarks of Bantam Books, Inc.

Cover photograph by Chuck Bell / The Studio Inc.
Cover inset photograph by Dan Morrill.
Author photograph courtesy of Harry Langdon Photography.

Library of Congress Cataloging-in-Publication Data

Zi, Nancy.
The art of breathing.

1. Breathing exercises.   2. Vitality.   I. Title.
RA782.Z5   1986   613'.192   85-90475
ISBN 0-553-34281-9

Published simultaneously in the United States and Canada

Bantam Books are published by Bantam Books, Inc. Its trademark, consisting of the words "Bantam Books" and the portrayal of a rooster, is Registered in U.S. Patent and Trademark Office and in other countries. Marca Registrada. Bantam Books, Inc., 666 Fifth Avenue, New York, New York 10103.

PRINTED IN THE UNITED STATES OF AMERICA

*This book is dedicated
to my mother,
Mrs. Lucy Ma Zi,
and my late father,
Reverend Benjamin Dung Hwe Zi*

Acknowledgments

I wish to express my deepest appreciation to Mr. Wang Chi-Chien for writing the calligraphic Chinese characters that so beautifully adorn the part openers of this book.

Mr. Ernie Pereira, managing editor of the *Hong Kong Standard* daily newspaper, gave me the first words of encouragement and guided me to write this book. I also wish to extend my thanks to Professor and Mrs. John Hsu of Cornell University, whose wise suggestions and careful scrutiny of the initial manuscript have led this book onto a much wiser course.

The invaluable artistic advice and other counsel of Mrs. Sue Yung Li Ikeda have guided me throughout this project.

I am also very grateful to my son, Vincent Li, and my daughter, Violette Li, for assisting in the preparation of the book.

It is my great fortune to have had the assistance of Charles Hammond and Margaret M. Meier in preparing the manuscript. I am also grateful to Eric Maché for his illustrations.

And finally, I cannot thank Alan Freeland and Kenneth Burke enough. Without them, this book would never have materialized in its present form.

Contents

List of Imagery Drills

THE ART OF
BREATHING

INTRODUCTION

A Singer's Discoveries

Breath is life; and learning to control the breath adds a new dimension of control and ease to every action, no matter how simple or how complex it is. In fact, the effectiveness of every activity we undertake—singing, walking, exercising, working, dancing, public speaking—depends greatly on how we use the air we breathe.

My voice is my career. For more than twenty years, much of my time has been devoted to singing and to voice instruction. My performance schedule is extensive and my teaching schedule full. I have to make certain that my singing voice is always in good condition and that my speaking voice does not strain my vocal cords. To maintain the quality of voice I desire, effective controlled breathing is my most important tool.

During my college days, at Millikin University in Illinois, I sang in student recitals and performed in many opera productions. Deep breathing automatically accompanied me whenever I stepped onstage to sing. Then, during my junior year, I was elected a candidate for Homecoming Queen. I will never forget the parade of candidates, each of us swiveling at center stage in front of a panel of judges. Suddenly I was like a lump of clay! What had happened to my customary poise and stage presence? Years later, the answer became clear to me. My breathing technique had eluded me, and without it I also lost my vibrancy and the ability to project my personality.

In the years that followed, I learned to apply the lesson of that experience: Deep breathing can get me through most situations.

Controlled deep breathing helps the body to transform the air we breathe into energy. The stream of energized air produced by properly executed and controlled deep breathing produces a current of inner energy which radiates throughout the entire body and can be channeled to the body areas that need it the most, on demand. It can be used to fuel a specific physical effort, such as tennis or jogging. Or you can use this current of inner energy to relieve muscular tension throughout the body, revitalize a tired mind, or soothe localized aches and pains.

My years of experience in training and maintaining the human voice have convinced me that the practice of the art of breathing is beneficial to the health of the whole person, regardless of career or activity. In this book I will share with you some of the discoveries I have made as a singer and voice teacher. These experiences have made me aware of the wide applications of disciplined, effective breathing.

As my understanding of the benefits of controlled breathing developed, I began to formulate the principles of what I call *chi yi*. *Chi* means breath, air, atmosphere. *Yi* means art. Hence *chi yi*—the art of breathing.

Chi yi (pronounced *chee ee*), the breathing method I have developed, is influenced in part by the basic principles of the ancient Chinese art of breath manipulation known as *chi kung* (pronounced *chee gung*). For centuries, the Chinese have practiced *chi kung* as a fundamental discipline, and have applied this discipline to many forms of martial arts, meditation, and healing practices. As a Western-trained singer and as a researcher and practitioner of the ancient art of *chi kung* and its related disciplines, I have compared, extracted, and compiled techniques from both East and West to create *chi yi*, a direct and concise way to teach the art of breathing. The current of inner energy that is generated as a result of my method of deep breathing is comparable to the principle of "inner vigor" upon which *chi kung* is based.

The practice of *chi kung* is concerned not only with the process of breathing; it also encompasses the ancient Chinese understanding of disciplined breathing as a means of acquiring total control over body and mind. It gives us physiological and psychological balance and the balance of *yin* and *yang*—a symbolic expression of such universal polarities as masculine and feminine, light and dark, creative and receptive. In *chi yi*, that energy is manifested through the manipulation of simultaneous inward and outward muscular pressure, thus creating opposing forces. By properly balancing these forces, we allow energy to emerge.

The ancient practitioners of *chi kung* further associated the inner energy that derives from disciplined breathing with the quality and vigor of the blood. They deduced ways to control and regulate the seemingly automatic breathing function, which they saw as voluntary. By deliberately controlling the breathing process, they found that other functions of the body—heartbeat, blood flow, and many other physical and emotional functions—could be consciously altered. The mind, said *chi kung* practitioners, can control and manipulate the flow of energy that is created through proper breathing. Therefore the mind, coordinated with breathing, can be responsible for the state of one's physical health, one's blood pressure, one's immune system, and one's mental condition. A *chi kung* expert can channel the inner energy to any location in the body at will. In other words, the accomplished practitioner can "think" this inner energy to any destination in the body where it is needed.

As time went on, the philosophical aspect of *chi kung* was explored in many books, but the technical aspect was treated as a closely guarded secret. Without documentation, the words of generations of teachers and pupils varied greatly in interpretation and practice. Therefore, while *chi kung* became the foundation that teaches the manipulation of body, mind, and spirit, different schools evolved that built upon this foundation yet had very different goals. *Tai chi* and other forms of the martial arts and meditation disciplines are all related to *chi kung*.

Centuries passed, and with the advent of machinery and explosive weapons, the martial arts waned in appeal. External sources of strength and power totally overshadowed the internal energy men and women had once learned to create within their own bodies through self-discipline. The specific talent for energizing the body through disciplined breathing was neglected and nearly forgotten. Western modernization seemed to have eclipsed many of the subtle practices of the East. Today, however, a new era of physical awareness has stimulated the reexamination of Eastern culture, with its foundation based on the importance of the inner self.

In effective breathing, of course, there is no East or West. True, different cultures have placed different degrees of emphasis on the importance and development of breathing, and have called their techniques by different names. Their ultimate objective, however, is the same: to derive the maximum efficiency from the inhaled breath.

My intention in *The Art of Breathing* is not to revive or to propagate *chi kung* but to bring attention to and illustrate the existence of the power that is ours if we choose to have it. By cultivating that power through the practice of *chi yi*, we can excel in our endeavors and become more successful and dynamic people. The exercises, applications of *chi yi* principles, and imagery drills described in this book will enable you to build a solid, deep, effective breathing system to support whatever activities you pursue.

PART ONE

The Promise of Chi Yi

Chi Yi: An Art for Today

The newborn infant gasps for its first breath, and life ends with a final exhalation. But breathing is more than just an instinct that is active from birth to death. When properly executed, breathing can help you develop to the utmost, enabling you to acquire a greater sense of power and balance and to sharpen both your mental and physical coordination. This is the promise of *chi yi*.

The demands of today's society, working conditions, and environment are complicated and frequently stressful; and our energy needs, both physical and mental, are forced to change rapidly to cope with all the forms of tension to which we are subjected. Innumerable varieties of relaxation techniques—transcendental meditation, self-hypnosis, physical exercises, biofeedback, and many others—are available today. But no matter what method is practiced, a mode of breathing in one way or another always comes into the picture.

Modern science has done wonders to elevate the standard of human existence, with the expectation that new inventions and medical discoveries will raise our physical and mental well-being to ever-higher states. Advanced education systems sharpen our minds, while vitamins and nutritional supplements ensure that our bodies are well nourished. Great efforts are devoted to developing innumerable variations of exercises that promise to enhance our physical shape and condition. All these avenues for generating and maintaining a high level of energy are pursued with the intention of producing a better, more exciting person.

Ironically, in our search for energy resources to maintain this modern lifestyle, we have overlooked the potential of the greatest energy source available to everyone: the current of vital energy that can be generated within our bodies, using the air we breathe as fuel. The Chinese call that energy *chi*.

Chi yi is a method of deep breathing through which you can stimulate and harness the current of inner energy. By making sure that the air you breathe is effectively inhaled, energized, and exhaled, you can improve your health and bring vitality to all your physical movements and expressions.

We have all experienced the direct link between our breathing and the way we feel physically and emotionally. We speak of a sigh of relief, of gasping in horror, of holding the breath in anticipation, of being breathless with excitement. Laughing, sighing, yawning, yelling, gasping, screaming—nature provides us with all these responses to help us fulfill the emotional demands of the instant. Physically, these acts provide us with the extra oxygen to meet a potential need.

These outbursts stimulate deep breathing—breathing to the "core"—in effect opening up vents to release emotional steam. In the next section, we will look at the core of our bodies— what it is, where it is located, and its role in effective breathing.

The Core

As you learn to apply the principles of *chi yi*, you will develop your core, and you will learn how to lead the breath to the point where the core is located. Your stresses, worries, anger, and other tensions will follow the stream of your breath to this center, where the core will shrink away your negative emotions—pain, fear, anxiety, anger, sadness, and even depression—leaving you ready to meet the challenges that you face.

To understand that a central core exists within all human beings is to open your eyes to a whole new dimension of your being. The core has always been within you. When it is stimulated it becomes increasingly effective. It does not grow in size, but in intensity.

The core is located at the center of the body, measuring from head to toe. That point is located approximately 2 to 5 inches below the navel (see Figure 1). The entire body is coordinated from this center of balance. In fact, this core is the center not only of your physical balance but of your mental and emotional balance as well.

The core thrives on attention and stimulation. The more you practice breathing to the core, the more energy it stores and is prepared to release, thus becoming a stronger pivot point for your physical, mental, and emotional balance and control.

In times of emotional crisis or at other crucial moments of distress or physical pain, we frequently hear the advice, "Take a deep breath and get hold of yourself." A very wise suggestion indeed, if we only knew how to make that "deep breath" effective. Expanding the chest and attempting to fill the lungs with additional air isn't necessarily helpful; the goal is to direct air deep toward the core.

It is impossible to explain in scientific terms the process of breathing to the core. Like energy, the core of a person is an abstract entity. Through exercises and imagery drills we can sense it, develop and cultivate it, manipulate it, and feel the power of its presence, but we cannot see it with our eyes.

Introducing the Imagery Drills

The following exercises are the first of several "imagery drills," which make use of mental pictures to help you experience specific sensations or feelings in the body. These mental pictures are metaphorical descriptions of particular movements that may be otherwise impossible to describe. They communicate a muscular process indirectly, through the use of *images* of movement. Such images are useful in elucidating invisible, internal movements and subtle adjustments of the body. This brief introduction to the awareness of inner energy merely suggests the energy source you will learn to tap in the exercises and applications that follow.

These imagery drills may be difficult for those who are unaccustomed to manipulating their breathing apparatus. Many athletes, singers, and musicians who play wind instruments, for example, are conscientious breathers, and will be able to handle the drills easily. Others will need to wait until they have practiced a good number of the exercises in Part 2 before being able to complete the drills correctly and with little strain.

Practice these drills as they are introduced to become familiar with the internal sensations each one stimulates. Review the drills as necessary to reestablish your awareness of a sensation.

The first of these drills, the Eyedropper Imagery Drill, introduces you to abdominal breathing, an important step in learning to breathe to the core at will.

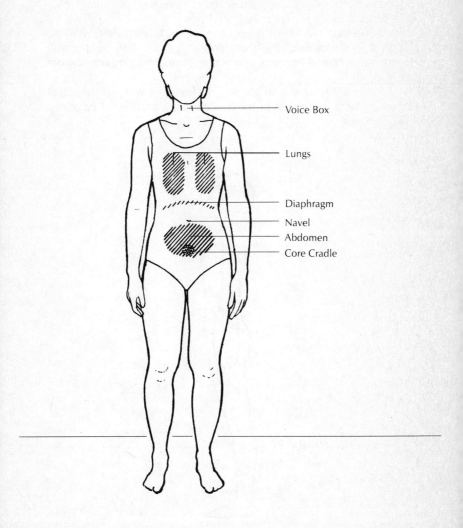

FIGURE 1 Breathing Apparatus

Eyedropper

Stand erect but relaxed, being careful not to tilt or lower your head. Imagine yourself to be an upside-down eyedropper (see Figure 2). Squeeze the bulb, and air is squeezed out. Release the bulb, letting it expand, and air is drawn into the body.

Imagine that the opening tip of the glass tube ends where the back of the nose and the throat meet. Let air flow in and out through this central opening, not simply through the mouth or nose alone.

Practice applying this image as you breathe. You will find that breathing with this image in mind encourages abdominal breathing very naturally.

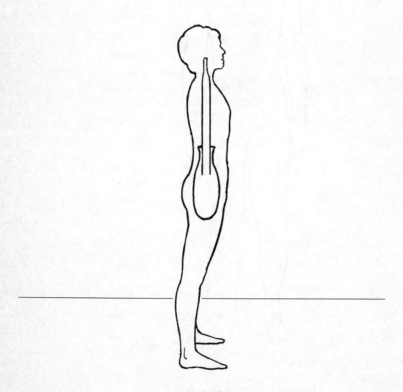

FIGURE 2 Eyedropper

Abdominal breathing does not mean that air enters into the abdomen but rather that the abdominal muscles and the sides and back of the lower torso expand outward to induce the lowering of the diaphragm, thus creating the appearance of an inflated abdomen.

The diaphragm is the main muscle used in breathing (see Figure 1); when it lowers, air is drawn into the lungs. On inhalation, air travels through the nose or mouth to the lungs, passing through the windpipe, which divides into two main bronchial tubes, one going into each lung. Oxygen in the inhaled air is transferred by the lungs to the blood, to be carried to the body tissues. Carbon dioxide, which is formed in this process, is carried by the blood back to the lungs and exhaled.

A simple inhalation of air containing oxygen cannot produce the phenomenal volume, extended range of pitches, and varied sounds and color that are demanded of a singer, nor the force and coordination demanded in the *grand jeté* of a classical dancer. The compounded energy that is developed in the body of the singer or dancer is comparable to the inner energy produced in *chi kung* to attain physical and mental well-being. The former focuses this current of energy outward, whereas the latter circulates it internally.

To further understand abdominal breathing, practice creating the mental image described in the following drill.

IMAGERY DRILL

Accordion

Create the mental image of the diaphragm as a ceiling resting on the abdominal walls (see Figure 3). Imagine that these walls and the ceiling are made of rubber that can be flexed and expanded.

From another perspective, the diaphragm is also a floor on which the lungs rest. Imagine the lungs to be a vertically held accordion. When the diaphragm drops, the accordion elongates, creating a vacuum space that sucks in air.

The whole breathing process can be summarized in this way: Expand your abdomen by curving the downstairs walls outward, causing the downstairs ceiling to lower and the upstairs floor to drop, thereby creating more space on top into which air can flow.

This image will help you to perceive how the abdomen, the lungs, and your exhalations/inhalations interact. In this drill, air is drawn in easily to fill the entire lung, and we have the illusion of air being drawn into the abdomen. In spite of its seeming simplicity, this drill demands the coordination of a juggling act. A central pivot point of control is necessary, and that is the core.

Once you are familiar with the existence and location of the core, you can stimulate it regularly and frequently with proper deep breathing. When the core is energized, all of your mental and physical performances will improve. This improvement comes not merely from being sufficiently energized but also from being able to relax unwanted muscular tension. The core works as a hub with spokes reaching out to the extremities, and the entire body can be saturated with its vibrant energy. Stress and tension can be transferred down those spokes to the core, where they can be converted into useful energy.

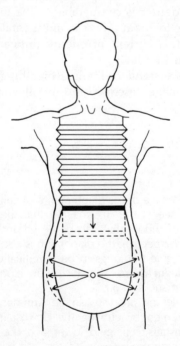

FIGURE 3 Accordion

Now practice the following imagery drills to help you get in touch with the core energy.

Funnel-Balloon

Think of the very back of your nose, where it meets the throat, as the top of a funnel. As you begin an inhalation, imagine the air you breathe as water being poured into this funnel, which leads all the way down to the end of a very long tube.

Imagine a balloon attached to the end of this tube. As you inhale easily and steadily, picture water draining down, and imagine the balloon slowly inflating. Be careful not to overfill and burst the balloon. Stop when it is comfortably full. Hold the inhaled air in the balloon for a second or so, enjoying and dwelling on that pleasant fullness. Now prepare for exhalation.

As you gradually exhale, imagine the full balloon deflating slowly, being careful to let the balloon sit firmly in place until the very end of the exhalation. After several repetitions of this exhalation/inhalation process, you will feel warmth saturating your lower abdomen. You might even feel a throbbing or tingling sensation in other parts of your body, such as the area between your cheeks and the upper gum in your mouth, at the base of your neck, at your rib cage, and even at your kneecaps or fingertips.

Tumbling Pebble

To stimulate the sensation of activated inner energy in the lower abdomen, imagine a pebble about 1/2 inch in diameter at the center of your lower abdomen. Imagine it tumbling by its own power, over and over, slowly at first, then steadily, about one turn per second.

When you are comfortable with that sensation, you may imagine adding more pebbles to the original one, each turning and tumbling by its own power.

Eventually, with practice of these and later imagery drills, you will be mentally able to stimulate the sensation of *activated inner energy*. This mental stimulation is vital in order to attain the maximum benefits from your study of *chi yi*.

The Benefits of Chi Yi

Breathing is a natural reflex. So why fuss about it? If we breathe normally, some say, that's good enough. If we follow this line of thinking, we might also ask: If we can stand on our feet, why practice dancing on tiptoe? Why develop *any* special techniques and abilities if we are meant only to do things easily and naturally? Human beings have developed thousands of exceptional abilities and talents. We develop ourselves in order to be more functional, more wholesome, and more effective.

Among its many benefits, the technique of *chi yi* brings to its practitioners:

☐ The ability to generate inner energy.

☐ The ability to channel this inner energy selectively.

☐ The ability to respond wisely to mental and physical needs.

The core's potential is limitless. The power that comes from core development through *chi yi* will influence every aspect of your daily life—mental and physical health, energy level, personality, voice, coordination, deportment, and many other interrelated activities and characteristics. Through *chi yi*, shyness and timidity can gradually diminish, permitting your full personality to emerge. Your mental and physical movements will find a common center of gravity, and the resulting coordination produces poise, grace, and ease.

In the final section of the book you will learn that *chi yi* has practical applications in relaxation, revitalization, improving your health, reducing or eliminating stress, tension, or pain anywhere in the body, combatting insomnia, developing your athletic prowess, and much more. For now, the following section gives a preview of the benefits you may expect.

Building Confidence and Enhancing Personal Presence

In this society of keen competition and the pursuit of excellence, a person must have that extra something in order to succeed. Especially in the fields of artistic and athletic performance, a fully functioning core gives you just that—an extra, indefinable *something*.

You will learn to incorporate an awareness of your core into every sound, motion, and emotion you express: breathing, speaking, smiling, walking, running, waving, and so on. From your inner depth you will exude sincerity, conviction, and strength. From the simplest to the most complex undertaking, you will benefit from this inner support. For example, the simple motion of lifting a teacup, when performed with an awareness of and coordination extending from the core, will be noticeably more steady, graceful, and spontaneous. Similarly, a deep breath flowing from your innermost center to your face will bring a luminous, captivating glow to your complexion.

In any stage performance, alone or in collaboration with others, a successful performer, in addition to possessing talent and mastery of the required skill, must exude a captivating force that propels his or her presence into the audience. This force, often called *stage presence*, is useful to performers and public figures—and to you when you wish to command attention and project an impressive self-image. An effective core can supply this force.

Increasing Stamina, Zest, and Coordination

If you are active in a sport—whether it's tennis, swimming, figure skating, jogging, or aerobic exercise—proper deep breathing can conspicuously improve your performance. With an awareness of the core and the use of its energy, your muscles and nervous system will become more responsive, controlled, and coordinated. This awareness enhances the execution of intricate, exacting movements. You will also be able to channel your energy more effectively, resulting in increased stamina and a higher tolerance for physical exertion.

By visualizing the location of your core, you establish a focal point from which to direct your movements. Imagine that all your limbs are connected to the core, and that all your movements extend from the core. You will quickly recognize the greater sense of coordination this visualization creates, even in a simple movement such as a jumping jack.

Exhalation channels the core's energy into the execution of energetic movements. This is one of the reasons that karate students are taught to emit vocal outbursts when attacking. Some tennis players such as John McEnroe, Chris Evert Lloyd, and Jimmy Connors frequently grunt with their most powerful hits—a verbal response as they use the inner energy tapped from exhalation.

As you work with the exercises, applications, and drills in this book, you will discover some breathing approaches that are particularly effective for you. Practice a few of these before you engage in your favorite sport. Work on breathing deeply and developing core energy, and see what a difference they make to your performance.

Improving the Complexion

Chi yi stimulates the flow of inner energy, bringing a vibrant glow to the surface of the skin. During the process of stimulating the core with deep breathing, the abdominal muscles flex, knead, and squeeze the organs of the abdomen, producing a massaging effect. This motion, together with activated inner energy, stimulates digestion and helps to relieve uncomfortable internal air bubbles and gas, promoting a clearer, brighter complexion. In addition, the nerve-calming effect of deep breathing will help to control the tension that is so frequently the primary cause of a bad complexion.

Freshening the Breath

Bad breath (halitosis), the kind that persists even though all hygienic precautions and proper eating habits are followed, can be helped through *chi yi* in several ways. Bad breath caused by an acidic stomach resulting from tension can be eased by relaxation through breathing. Bad breath resulting from indigestion may be eliminated through the abdominal stimulation brought on by deep breathing and inner energy. Bad breath caused by shallow breathing that traps stagnant air in the lungs can easily be remedied with a replenishing deep-breathing technique.

Preparing for Childbirth

If you are an expectant father who is also a practitioner of *chi yi*, you will be able to calm your own tensions over the next nine months with deep breathing, and you will be well prepared to assist in the delivery of your child by guiding the breathing of the mother.

If you are an expectant mother who has already learned the techniques of *chi yi*, your abdominal muscles are strong and healthy—elastic and responsive. Your breathing is efficient and easy to manipulate. You are sure to benefit from these assets during your pregnancy. These qualities are also a great advantage during the delivery, when your baby—and your doctor—will need all the physical cooperation you can give. Not only will your ability to breathe effectively keep you healthier mentally and emotionally during pregnancy, your baby will benefit from your inner energy too.

If you are planning to use the Psychoprophylactic Method, a psychological and physical preparation for childbirth known also as the Lamaze Method, or any other method of natural childbirth, you will find that your ability in *chi yi* is extremely helpful in learning and carrying out these techniques. All such methods require you to train your breathing to suit the stages of delivery—dilation, transition, and expulsion. With *chi yi*, you are already expert in the control of exhalations and inhalations and in maneuvering their rate, duration, and intensity.

During the prenatal and postpartum periods, numerous physical exercises will probably be prescribed for you to help with your delivery and recovery. Explicit breathing instructions are seldom supplied with these exercises. If you already practice disciplined deep breathing, your ability to incorporate effective breathing into the exercises will greatly increase their beneficial results.

If you have never practiced *chi yi* before, you should consult your doctor before beginning these exercises during pregnancy. Every woman's physical condition varies, and every pregnancy has its own characteristics. For most normal pregnancies, the practice of *chi yi* should be helpful, whether you are a beginner or an experienced practitioner. Moderation must be observed, and your doctor's advice must always take priority. Even through the later part of your pregnancy, your doctor will most likely not object to your continuing with *chi yi*. As with swimming, tennis, and other forms of physical exercise and training, if you have been accustomed to doing it all along, there should be no harm in its continuance during a normal pregnancy.

Madame Ernestine Schumann-Heink, a famed contralto of the late nineteenth and early twentieth centuries, had many children. She was almost constantly pregnant during the prime of her career, and if she had stopped singing during her pregnancies, she would have had no career at all. Her biographers say that she performed almost up to the week of delivery and was back on stage again a few weeks after, breastfeeding her babies backstage between acts. Her breathing practice as a singer must surely have prepared her for such a devoted approach to child rearing.

Relieving Aches, Pains, and Discomforts

Aches and pains and other discomforts can arise for numerous reasons, and you should consult your physician about them if they are serious. However, if the doctor simply prescribes temporary relief such as painkillers, tranquilizers, or decongestants, you can supplement these medications with the inner energy cultivated from the practice of *chi yi*. Pains due to tension, rheumatic and arthritic pains, and lower back pain may be eliminated or greatly eased by channeling core energy to soothe the painful area.

Hastening Convalescence

For those who are convalescing or receiving physical therapy, *chi yi* can offer assistance.

An elderly friend of mine had been hospitalized for several weeks. At home again, she told me that the doctor had ordered her to get out of bed and start moving around, but she could not. She felt too weak even to sit up. I suggested that she should get up while I was visiting, first taking a few deep breaths to muster up some energy. She insisted that she could barely breathe, let alone breathe deeply. I pressed my palm firmly over her lower abdomen. As intended, my palm pressure felt heavy to her, and her abdominal muscle pushed slightly against my hand. If she could resist my palm pressure once, I told her, she could do the same a few more times with more strength.

As she did so, I asked her to synchronize her abdominal movements with her inhalation. "This is abdominal deep breathing," I told her, and she was amazed and encouraged by her accomplishment.

After she had relaxed awhile, I again called her attention to her breathing. This time I pressed against her abdomen with only my middle finger. Then I suggested that she should get up. I asked her to imagine the sensation of my finger pressing continuously against her abdomen: She could focus on that spot and from it draw all the energy she needed to stand up. With a minimum of help from her nurse, she sat up in bed, lifted her feet, and placed them on the floor. Our first goal was accomplished when she stood up by herself and slowly took a few steps to her easy chair. Her rapid recovery from then on amazed not only herself but her doctor as well, as she continued to practice this *chi yi* technique.

Certain *chi yi* exercises can be modified to fit the requirements of convalescence or disability. If you are recovering from a leg injury and are unable to stand, for example, you can execute the standing exercises and applications in this book in a sitting position. If part of your body is in a cast and cannot be moved or bent, you can still practice your breathing by eliminating the impossible motions and striking the postures indicated in the exercise or application as nearly as you can. Sensibly modified exercises and applications are still effective. Most people under physical restraint will pamper the injured area by keeping it immobile. In restricting movement, they also are likely, unconsciously, to restrain their breathing, causing it to be shallow. This limited intake of air reduces stimulation to the core and cuts down the supply of inner energy that is so necessary for recovery and healing.

Minimizing the Effects of Aging

Many people at an advanced age are suddenly confronted with the fact that their health and their very existence could have been greatly enhanced if they had put their lungs to fuller use. Shortness of breath, tight aching chest muscles, an uninspiring voice, tension, the heaving of shoulders in a useless effort to overcome the insufficient inhalation of air—all of these problems are frequently caused by poor breathing habits.

Aging is an unavoidable process characterized by the gradual loss of strength, energy, and coordination. The effects of such physical degeneration can be retarded or minimized through the development and use of core energy. Instead of fumbling aimlessly for the strength to lift yourself up, move, or walk, seek that needed strength at your core. The next time you feel too tired to stand up from sitting or stooping, visualize inward, take a deep breath, and lift up from your core as you stand. You will discover how effortless that movement can be.

Much of the image of aging is reflected in one's movement and carriage. To be able to stand more erect and to move more briskly will help you to look and feel younger.

Inner energy in a person can be likened to the electric current in a battery. When you are young, you are more fully charged, and as you proceed in life, unless you know how to recharge your inner battery, your inner energy circulation decreases steadily. When the inner energy loses some of its power and is no longer functioning at full capacity, the current will gradually withdraw, first from the farthest extremities, such as fingers, hands, and feet, and then from the arms and legs.

The joints, like the elbows in plumbing where clogging tends to occur, will also suffer from this insufficient supply of inner energy. As you grow older, you are likely to be plagued with aches and pains in these extremities—painful knuckles, aching feet, tennis elbow, and charley horses, to name a few. Any part of your body may be deprived of a sufficient supply of this inner current, leaving you unable to ward off or overcome invading illnesses.

If, when you are young and healthy, you have the foresight to develop and practice the skill of regularly generating inner energy, you will avoid the rapid decline of your inner energy stockpile. For the young of today, who frequently burn their candles at both ends, it is especially important to ensure that the supply of inner energy is not depleted but is replaced steadily. For those who are not so young, too, the supply of inner energy can be rapidly replenished and its circulation restored.

Improving Speech and Voice

No other human activity is more influenced by breathing than vocalization. Proper breathing, supported by a healthy core, will ease tension in the vocal apparatus, which is the usual cause of raspiness, hoarseness, squeakiness, breathiness, breathlessness, weakness, nasality, and many other impediments to clear speech. To mend and strengthen a misused, ailing, or underdeveloped voice, you must begin by making sure that the air you take in is correctly inhaled, energized, and exhaled.

Singing, especially classical singing, is a much more intense and demanding form of vocalization than is speech. It is an exaggerated form of elongated speech with built-in self-amplication and with extended range. In addition to musical intelligence and talent, a proficient singer needs extensive and intensive training and practice to master such intricate vocal execution. The singer must above all acquire the important technique of breath support.

When breath support is insufficient for a desired volume, inflection, or tone, whether in singing or in speech, we automatically supplement the missing energy by tensing up the chest, shoulder, or neck muscles, or all of them. But using rigid vocal cords can damage them, leading to functional problems such as soreness, breathiness, raspiness, hoarseness, loss of voice, and even the developing of nodes.

Breath is the foundation on which the voice is built, and it is only sensible to develop a reliable breathing skill, a skill that will provide sufficient energy and control for vocal support.

The image our speaking voice creates is just as important as our physical appearance. Our character, personality, state of mind, and degree of charisma are judged by how we sound. It is also true that how one sounds is related to how one looks.

Energetic, expressive speech generates obvious excitement in the listener, but a raspy, breathless, tired voice can blemish the most attractive appearance. Correct breathing is an essential component of good speech. With the help of deep breathing, a damaged voice can usually be mended. Speech defects can be smoothed out. The tone, the color, the ease, the contour of a voice can be developed. An average voice can be improved. A good voice can become more polished and perfected.

The voice possesses the unique power to express emotions through the laws of exclamatory vowels that are common to all human beings. Although the meanings of "ah," "oh," and "ee" may vary from culture to culture, their use is universal. Pitch denotes degrees of excitement. The depth of the breath relates to the depth of the vocal projection. The deeper the breath, the more thoroughly the feeling is released.

Every deep breath we take should give us a sense of well-being and make us feel uplifted. The world grows brighter then, and we want to open up and sing. Singing is healthy. It invites us to control a flowing stream of air and to release any pent-up emotions.

Sing anywhere you can. Sing in the shower, sing in your garden, sing in the car on the way to work. Never mind if you are tone deaf and sing out of tune. Sing for yourself. Don't worry about who may hear you. Memorize the words to a few songs — pop, rock, folk songs, hymns, even your favorite operatic arias. Don't worry if you are no Enrico Caruso or Barbra Streisand; just sing freely, comfortably. If you forget the words, make them up, or sing "la-la-la-la." Don't be shy about hearing your own voice.

Gradually, your true expressive self will emerge. You may even surprise yourself as you hear improvements in your singing. As your breathing method improves through the practice of *chi yi*, your singing voice will improve too. Let it be a barometer of your progress in learning the art of breathing.

Focusing the Breath in Meditation

Through the centuries, Buddhist monks and meditators of many faiths and beliefs have practiced meditation as a means of ascending to higher mental and spiritual plateaus; and they have asserted that the key to successful meditation is proper manipulation of the breath.

The yogis of the Himalayas went further, maintaining that controlled alternate-nostril breathing is essential. They claimed that normal breathing has a natural cycle that alternates between emphasis on the left and right nostrils. The ancient yogis believed that right-nostril breathing induced more active and aggressive instincts, while breathing through the left made one more passive and subdued. This belief brings to mind recent research on the different functions performed by the right and left hemispheres of the brain.

The practice of *chi yi* techniques establishes for you the basic ability to advance into many forms of meditation. In the process of disciplining and controlling breathing, you direct your mental attention inward, thus minimizing or even eliminating external distractions. The ability to centralize and control all mental and physical awareness is the key to total self-control of the body and mind, which is basically what meditation is all about. *Chi yi* trains the mind's eye to look inward and remain in focus, bringing about a state of total relaxation.

The ability to control your own physical and mental state produces immense satisfaction. To lie in sleeplessness or pain without the ability to combat it undermines self-confidence. Being competent in *chi yi* makes the difference between being helpless and being in charge. Begin to learn *chi yi* today!

PART TWO

Exercises
for Practicing
Chi Yi

Some Suggestions for Practice

What follows is the heart of *chi yi* training. These are thirty exercises, arranged in six progressive lessons, to guide you toward increased awareness of proper breathing habits and greater control of your breath.

Although the theory is easily grasped, diligent practice is required for the muscles and nervous system to handle this new technique reflexively. Learning *chi yi* takes motivation, concentration, and persistence. Eventually, though, taking a shallow breath will require more effort than practicing deep breathing from the abdomen. As your awareness of the breathing process is developed through the exercises, you will soon find the principles of deep breathing moving into your daily activities until you, too, are an artist in the art of breathing.

The deep-breathing skills and the resulting energy to be gained from practicing these exercises can be applied in many ways, to both physical and mental tasks. They can supplement and enhance whatever special physical skill you may be pursuing—making a business presentation, dancing, acting, or general physical activities such as jogging, aerobic exercise, or golf.

Don't be discouraged if you feel lost during your initial attempts to capture certain sensations and physical controls. With careful repetition you will begin to feel and perform as described in this book. As *chi yi* becomes habitual, you will gain in stamina, grace, radiance, and general well-being.

To some readers the exercises in this book, especially those in the first few lessons, may seem overly simple. In fact, they are very demanding because they must be performed precisely. Each detail is directed to an important purpose. The purposes of each exercise may seem abstract at first, but with practice they will soon become evident.

Each of the six lessons takes about 10 to 20 minutes to complete, depending on how much rest you require between exercises. You may decrease the number of repetitions indicated in the exercises according to your endurance. When you first begin to practice controlled breathing, you may feel slightly dizzy. Pause to recover before proceeding. Dizziness may be a signal of overexertion. Take time out for a rest interval whenever you need one, even if no rest break is indicated in the exercise instructions. If you wish to increase the number of repetitions of a particular exercise, do so with caution and with sufficient rest between repetitions.

Dress comfortably to accommodate the various movements and positions called for in the exercises. Loose comfortable clothes are recommended. Avoid constricting collars, waistbands, or belts that might restrict free and easy breathing.

The exercises do not require a lot of space, but it is a good idea to practice in a place where you can concentrate and not be interrupted. You may practice either indoors or outdoors. You will find that a stuffy room is not conducive to the practice of *chi yi*, because after the first couple of minutes of deep breathing you will begin to feel uncomfortably warm. To achieve the maximum benefit from the exercises that follow, open a window or two; it is always revitalizing to inhale fresh air.

For the exercises that are performed lying down, you will need a mat or a carpeted floor. A bare floor is not comfortable, and a soft bed does not give enough support.

You may practice any time during the day or evening, but be sure to rest at least 15 to 20 minutes after practicing before eating a meal. Also wait an hour or two after a meal before practicing, depending on how heavy a meal you have eaten.

Practice each lesson twice daily in two separate sessions. Practice each lesson for at least three days to allow sufficient time to master the skills and for your muscles to develop progressively.

After practicing a lesson twice daily for at least three consecutive days, you are ready to move on to the next lesson. If you cannot always practice twice daily, but feel thoroughly confident in performing all of the exercises in a lesson, you may proceed to the next lesson after three days. If you have skipped practicing for an entire day, it is advisable to go over each exercise once (ignoring repetitions) in the old lesson before going on to the new one. If you have not practiced for more than two days, review the previous lesson or lessons for a day or two before proceeding. In any case, let your own feeling about your mastery of the material be your guide.

Deep breathing means exhalations and inhalations that fill the upper and the lower lungs, involving the muscles of the lower torso, including the front, sides, and lower back. It is necessary to develop and tone the muscles in these areas with exercises that will induce specific results at the appropriate time. Therefore it is important to follow closely all the details specified in the exercises.

We are used to thinking of breathing as a process of inhalation-exhalation, in that order of importance. We seldom give any thought to how we exhale. Most advice on breathing emphasizes inhalation, as in "take a deep breath." The truth is that exhalation is just as important. Exhalations are cultivated and refined inner energy being selectively channeled, the reaping of what we sow when we inhale.

Important: Although the *effects* of these exercises will eventually carry over into normal breathing, the exercises themselves are intended *only* as exercises. They should not be taken as substitute methods for normal, everyday breathing. The exercises are demanding and should not be overpracticed. If signs of dizziness or other discomfort occur, stop! You have done enough for the time being. Divert your attention away from breathing by attending to other activities. Your breathing will automatically return to its normal manner and you will recuperate quickly.

Counting

In exercises where a *slow count* is indicated, each count should be executed at the rate of approximately one per second.

The numbers specified for counting mentally as we breathe are not picked arbitrarily but are chosen to gauge the duration of exhalations and inhalations under specific conditions. However, you will notice a pattern that persists throughout the book: Inhalations end with odd numbers, and exhalations end with even numbers. A psychological reason guides this usage. Most people count in pairs: At an odd number, we are mentally prepared to proceed and are therefore anticipating; at an even number we are more inclined to stop. When we end an inhalation, it is beneficial to feel anticipation and movement, whereas when we end an exhalation, it is preferable to experience a feeling of completion.

Posture

Observe the following points as you practice the exercises:

☐ Proper posture encourages proper breathing.

☐ The shoulders must never be raised or tightened. They should be relaxed and uninvolved during both exhalation and inhalation.

☐ The chest must never feel depressed or sunken.

As you sit, stand, or walk, stay erect, being careful not to stick out behind. Your head should be held straight and upright on an imaginary line drawn from the tailbone to the center top of the head. A tilted or lowered head tightens the muscles under the chin and neck, obstructing the free flow of the stream of breath.

The angle of the pelvis is essential for maintaining good posture. When you tilt your pelvis by lifting the pubic bone up in front, the abdominal and buttocks muscles are best able to support the trunk, and strain on your lower back is minimized. To further minimize straining, practice the following imagery drill.

IMAGERY DRILL

String of Beads

Imagine that your body parts are beads of different shapes. Attach a string to the floor, and string the beads. After the final bead (representing the head) is put on, pull the string taut and straight upward. All the beads should fall perfectly into place in a straight line. The different parts of your body should feel like beads on a string—well aligned, with all parts properly positioned and in place.

After a lifetime of shallow breathing, the top portion of the lungs has had more use and is stretched more than the bottom portion. We need not further emphasize the development of this top portion. On the contrary, this portion of the lungs should be left alone. Any attempt to emphasize its use will distract from and impede the development of the lower portion. Eventually, when the level of functional ability and elasticity of the lower lungs matches that of the top, both will automatically function together as a whole.

If you have ever blown up a long balloon, you will remember that balloons of this shape inflate easily only at the end where air enters. Unless you manipulate the balloon, the far end will scarcely inflate at all. You may have noticed that after several tries the inflated end becomes much looser and more elastic than the other end, creating an even greater tendency toward one-ended inflation. One trick to overcome this situation is to stretch and pull the far end of the balloon manually, loosening up the far end before inflating it.

The lungs are like this long balloon. Due to a variety of physical circumstances the bottom part of the lungs, like the far end of the balloon, is hardly used. Unless we do something about shallow breathing, the lungs will become increasingly top-heavy as we grow older. The progressive exercises in this book will deter this unhealthy condition. You will frequently hear elderly—and sometimes not so elderly—people complaining about the difficulty of breathing. Often this condition arises as the top part of the lungs becomes overburdened and overused and loses its elasticity, while the lower part of the lungs is undeveloped and incapable of undertaking its share of the lungs' function. It is never too late to begin training your lower lungs to be functional through the practice of *chi yi*.

Developing Internal Sensations and Muscular Controls

As you practice each of the exercises in the upcoming six lessons, try to maintain your awareness of the following sensations and means of muscular control. *Refer frequently to these two lists to increase your awareness of these qualities.*

Internal Sensations

☐ Be conscious of the *lower abdominal area*, located below the navel, which is inflatable and deflatable.

☐ Experience the sensation of breath flowing into and inflating the *lower abdomen* during inhalation.

☐ Experience the sensation of the deflation of the *lower abdomen* during exhalation.

☐ Experience a mental image and the sensation of the *tongue* extending from the tip to its root, not ending at the throat or the neck or the chest but extending all the way down to the pit of the stomach.

☐ As the tip of the *tongue* touches the back of the top front teeth during inhalation, imagine the tongue as a conduit. Air travels along this conduit from the nostrils past the tip of the tongue and flows all the way down to the tongue's root. At this point the stream of air loops around and travels back up and out.

☐ Experience the sensation of the *tongue's* relaxed positions. The tongue should feel limp and relaxed, not a tight lump or an inflexible strip. A tense tongue can cause tension in the neck, chest, and shoulder muscles, restricting the free flow of air into the lower abdomen.

☐ Experience the sensation of stimulating the *tongue's root* so that it more fully participates in the visible tongue's control and movement. Elongation, movement, and relaxation of the visible part of the tongue establishes sensation in the root and reinforces your ability to relocate tongue tension to the core as you breathe abdominally.

☐ Whenever "hold breath" is indicated between inhalation and exhalation, create a sensation of that breath continuously sinking and settling down to the bottom of the *abdomen* during the "hold" period.

☐ During exhalation, create a sensation of air being drained through a hole in the bottom of the *abdomen*.

☐ Experience the yawning sensation (at the *back of the throat* and the adjoining *nasal passage*) that creates a central opening for the flow of air.

Muscular Controls

☐ Proper opening of the mouth for exercise will be attained only if the *jaws* are opened in a rounded "reclining U" shape (⊂), not in an angular "reclining V" shape (<). To achieve this, stretch the jaws open not only in front but all the way back to the jaw hinges so that the top and bottom molars form an almost parallel line.

☐ Be sure to breathe freely as you practice the exercises that emphasize your *neck muscles.*

☐ Produce a *steady stream of breath* instead of disjointed short puffs.

☐ Movements of the arms, legs, spine, neck, and so on should be initiated by inner energy from the *lower abdomen.*

☐ Strengthen the *lower abdominal muscles* by expanding outward and pulling inward at will, with or without breathing.

☐ Use your fingertips and palms to assist and monitor the movements of the *abdominal muscles* whenever necessary.

LESSON ONE

Leading the Breath

Lesson 1 introduces a natural, simple, and effective method of breath discipline. The four exercises in Lesson 1 are designed to stretch your abdominal and lower back torso muscles. These muscles are among the principal elements involved in the kind of deep breathing that comes so naturally to healthy infants and is often lost as we grow older.

Through neglect and lack of exercise, the muscles of the abdominal wall and the lower back torso become rigid and unresponsive. Another factor in the avoidance of diaphragmatic deep breathing is the cultural attitude that regards protrusion of the abdomen as unfashionable. These and other properly designed breathing exercises do not make the stomach muscles protrude. On the contrary, development of these muscles reduces flabbiness, adds strength and elasticity, and increases your ability to hold your stomach in when you desire to do so.

Lesson 1 also helps you to develop your awareness of the yawning sensation at the back of the nose and throat that you achieve when inhaling. This sensation, which is emphasized in the Eyedropper Imagery Drill, induces the nose-throat junction to act as a wide funnel for the deep, free flow of air.

Once you are familiar with the exercises, the first lesson can be completed in 5 to 10 minutes, but be careful not to rush the exercises, or to skip any steps. This first lesson introduces movements and sensations that are essential to the lessons that follow. Practice it carefully twice a day for at least three days, until you feel comfortable with all the exercises.

EXERCISE 1

Stretching the Abdominal Muscles

In a sitting position, all muscles, especially those of the legs, are more relaxed. In this position you can readily focus your attention on the abdominal muscles.

Sitting straight is important in order to form a right angle at the torso-buttocks junction. This position gives the lower abdominal area a maximum spread upward, which in turn allows greater breath capacity.

1. Sit up straight in a chair with your feet on the floor 4 to 5 inches apart.

2. Place your hands against the lower abdominal wall with your palms inward, fingertips not quite meeting (see Figure 4).

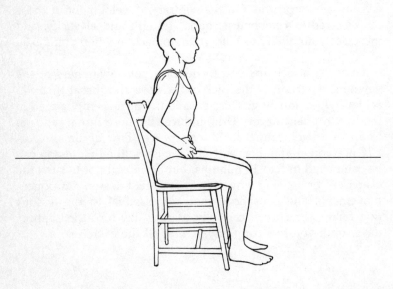

FIGURE 4

3. Place the tip of your tongue behind your bottom front teeth. Exhale through your mouth by blowing gently through slightly pursed lips to a slow count of 1-2-3-4-5-6. Begin the exhalation from the abdomen, simultaneously deflating the abdominal wall and adding inward pressure from the fingertips. On the sixth count, exert extra pressure to deflate the abdomen completely.

4. Place the tip of your tongue against the back of your top front teeth. Inhale through your nose as you create a yawning sensation in the back of the nose and throat to a slow count of 1-2-3-4-5-6-7. At the same time, expand the lower abdominal wall outward. On the seventh count, give the lower abdominal wall an extra push outward with an emphatic intake of breath to reach maximum expansion.

5. Without pausing, repeat the exhale-inhale sequence (steps 3 and 4) three times.

6. Relax.

7. Repeat the exhale-inhale sequence (steps 3 and 4) four times.

8. Relax for a few minutes before going on to Exercise 2.

EXERCISE 2

Stretching the Lower Back Muscles

When you bend over from a sitting position, the lower back muscles are stretched to their maximum length, and air can easily be inhaled to that area.

Holding your hands on your ankles with your elbows turned outward further encourages the spreading and extending of the lower back torso.

It is important to sit with your feet 8 to 10 inches apart. If the feet are too close together, the lower front abdominal muscle is restricted; if they are too far apart, the tailbone tends to stick out, resulting in a swayback that restricts the lower back muscles.

1. Sit up straight in a chair with your feet on the floor 8 to 10 inches apart. Place your hands in your lap, palms downward. Turn your palms inward with your thumbs toward your body, allowing your elbows to turn outward and forward. Gently grasp your upper thighs with your thumbs on the outside and your fingers on the inside of your thighs (see Figure 5).

2. Bend forward gradually while sliding your hands down your legs toward your ankles (see Figure 6). Firmly grasp the ankles (or the legs as close to the ankles as comfortably possible). Bend your head downward toward the floor, and turn your elbows farther out. In this position, focus your attention on your lower back and tailbone.

3. With your head still down, place the tip of your tongue behind your bottom front teeth. Exhale through your mouth by blowing gently through slightly pursed lips to a slow count of 1-2-3-4. At the same time, gradually deflate the lower abdominal wall.

4. Hold your breath, and remain still for 2 seconds.

5. Place the tip of your tongue against the back of your top front teeth. Inhale through your nose, creating a yawning

sensation at the back of the nose and throat, to a slow count of 1-2-3-4-5. Direct the air you are inhaling toward the base of your torso. Imagine elongating the spine as you inhale while inflating the lower back torso. On the fifth count, give both sides of the lower back torso an extra expansion outward with an emphatic intake of breath.

6. Hold your breath, and remain still for 3 seconds.

7. Repeat steps 1 through 6 four times.

8. Sit up very slowly. Exhale.

9. Relax for a few minutes before going on to Exercise 3.

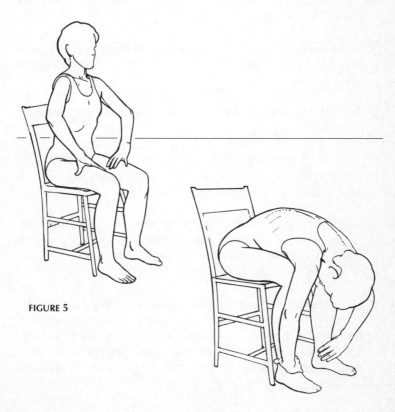

FIGURE 5

FIGURE 6

EXERCISE 3

Stretching the Muscles at the Base of the Torso

Spreading the knees as far apart as possible in a kneeling position expands the lower torso. This posture draws your attention to the lower abdominal muscles and focuses muscular activity at the point where inflating and deflating most effectively take place.

Sliding your hands downward while inhaling deters your shoulders from heaving and discourages air from flowing uncontrollably and exclusively into the upper torso. The aim of this movement is to fill the lower torso with breath first, and then gradually let the breath pile upward. The feeling of fullness of breath must progress from bottom to top without allowing the lower area to deflate.

1. Kneel with your back and upper legs straight and at a right angle to your lower legs, and with your toes pointing to the back.

2. Spread your knees as far apart as possible without bending your body.

3. Place your hands just above the hips with palms inward, fingers pointing downward, and thumbs forward. Spread your elbows to the sides (see Figure 7).

4. Place the tip of your tongue against your bottom front teeth. Exhale through your mouth by blowing gently through slightly pursed lips to a slow count of 1-2-3-4-5-6 while deflating the lower abdomen.

5. Place the tip of your tongue against your top front teeth. Inhale through your nose, creating a yawning sensation at the back of the nose and throat, to a slow count of 1-2-3-4-5-6-7. Simultaneously inflate the lower abdomen and slide your hands gradually down your thighs until your arms are straight (see Figure 8).

6. Place the tip of your tongue against your bottom front teeth. Exhale through your mouth to a slow count of 1-2-3-4-5-6 while pulling your hands gradually back up to their original upper-hip-level position and deflating the lower abdomen.

7. Repeat steps 5 and 6 three times.

8. Remaining in position, relax briefly.

9. Repeat steps 4 through 6 three times.

10. Sit back straight on your chair.

11. Relax for a few minutes before going on to Exercise 4.

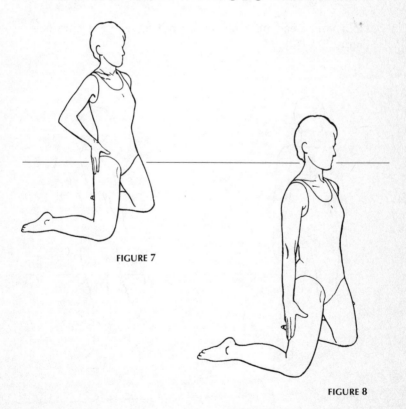

FIGURE 7

FIGURE 8

EXERCISE 4

Stretching the Lower Front and Back Torso

The standing position does not induce the stretching or flexing of your torso muscles. In this neutral position, a higher degree of mental control of abdominal and lower back muscles is required to achieve the desired physical effect.

Joining hands behind your back and pushing them downward prevents your shoulders from heaving as you extend the front torso. Bending down while exhaling assists the contraction of the lower front abdominal muscles. Then, as you return to the standing position while inhaling, the inhaled air flows easily into the lower front abdominal area.

1. Stand up straight with your feet 18 to 20 inches apart.

2. Hold your head up straight; do not lower your chin (see Figure 9).

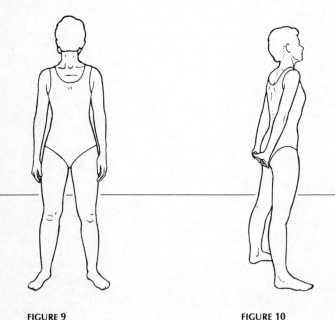

FIGURE 9   FIGURE 10

3. Join your hands together behind your back, palms down, locking your fingers.

4. Stretch your locked hands downward as far as possible, being careful not to stick your tailbone out and backward (see Figure 10).

5. Place the tip of your tongue against your bottom front teeth. Exhale through your mouth by blowing gently through slightly pursed lips to a slow count of 1-2-3-4-5-6 while gradually bending forward as far as possible and deflating the lower abdominal wall (see Figure 11).

6. Place the tip of your tongue against your top front teeth. Inhale through your nose, creating a yawning sensation at the back of your nose and throat, to a slow count of 1-2-3-4-5 while expanding the lower abdominal wall and returning to the original standing position, described in steps 1 through 4.

7. Repeat steps 5 and 6 five times.

8. Exhale, relax, and rest.

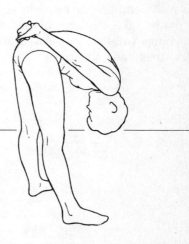

FIGURE 11

Thoughts on Lesson 1

The points made in Lesson 1 are simple, yet frequently the most obvious point may prove to be the one most easily overlooked. The most instinctive act, such as walking, frequently turns out to be difficult or even distorted.

Besides the objectives already discussed in Exercises 1 through 4 of Lesson 1, two very basic mental points must be introduced and established.

First, always think of the breath sequence as exhalation/inhalation instead of the reverse. At any relaxed instant, some air always remains in the lungs; by expelling this leftover air, you are ready to start your first conscious inhalation afresh.

Second, the outflowing and inflowing of air (exhalation and inhalation) should produce no audible sounds. The sounds of gasping can be very disruptive, and even annoying, especially in speakers, singers, and wind instrumentalists. The split seconds that are allowed for air intake between phrases of speech or music demand that you leave your nose and mouth openings unobstructed. If you think about drawing in air through these openings, the muscles in these areas will be tense and narrow. Instead, apply the mental picture described in the Eyedropper Imagery Drill. Let the air be drawn in by your lower abdomen (the rubber bulb, as you imagine it), simultaneously letting your nose-throat junction act as a passive receptacle, like the top of a funnel. The muscles in these openings will then be relaxed and stretchable, allowing air to flow freely and silently.

Coordinating the Breath

When your tongue is tense and pulled in an inflexible lump toward the back of the throat, it obstructs the free flow of the breath and impairs your speech. Tension in the tongue extends to the throat, shoulder, chest, and abdominal muscles, preventing inhaled air from flowing freely to the bottom of the lungs. The relaxed tongue is crucial to deep breathing.

A continuous muscular connection runs from the tip of the tongue to the pit of the stomach. By learning to relax the tip of the tongue, and to mentally relocate its tension to the core, you will learn to relieve the tension of the tongue and to stimulate the core as well.

Open your mouth wide when doing the tongue exercises in this lesson to give maximum room for free movement of the tongue and the breath. A very small proportion of people may have weak jaw hinge muscles, so be careful not to strain these muscles by performing overexaggerated jaw movements for an extended period of time. If you do strain your jaw hinges, gentle massage with the fingertips will bring instant relief.

REVIEW   EXERCISES 1, 2, AND 4 FROM LESSON 1

The review exercises are an integral part of the lessons. They are designed to fit into a group of exercises that are aimed at a specific purpose. As you do these exercises sequentially, you may become aware of the relationships among them. As you repeat them in the order given in the Review, you will be more aware of the cumulative nature of several exercises. The review of specific exercises, in a specific order, is also designed to strengthen your ability to perform them and to ease you into new exercises.

Review Exercises 1, 2, and 4 to recapture the sensations developed in Lesson 1. In doing Exercise 4, reduce the number of repetitions in step 7 from five to three. Then proceed to Exercise 5.

EXERCISE 5

Releasing Tongue Tension

This exercise stretches and extends the neck tendons and muscles and relieves any tension or kinks you may have.

Stretching your locked hands downward behind your back prevents your shoulders from heaving and inhibits inhaled air from flooding the upper torso and blocking the smooth flow of air into the lower abdomen.

If possible, perform Exercise 5 in front of a mirror; it is important to monitor the mouth and tongue positions closely. During this exercise, be sure you don't raise your shoulders while practicing the mouth and tongue movements. Your tongue should remain relaxed at all times.

1. Stand with your feet 10 to 12 inches apart.

2. Tilt your head back as far as possible; then bring it to an upright position in which it is tilted back slightly.

3. Join your hands together behind your back, locking your fingers.

4. Lower your locked hands to your buttocks, being careful not to stick your tailbone out and backward.

5. Open your mouth wide and touch your tongue to your top front teeth at a point about 1/2 to 3/4 inch in from the tip of your tongue (see Figure 12).

6. Inhale through your mouth to a slow count of 1-2-3 while inflating the lower abdomen.

7. Place the tip of your relaxed tongue behind your bottom front teeth (see Figure 13). Exhale through your mouth by blowing gently to a slow count of 1-2-3-4 while deflating the lower abdomen.

8. Once again, open your mouth wide and touch your tongue to your bottom front teeth at a point 1/2 to 3/4 inch in from the tip (see Figure 14).

9. Inhale through your mouth to a slow count of 1-2-3 while inflating the lower abdomen.

10. Place the tip of your tongue behind your bottom front teeth (see Figure 13). Exhale through your mouth to a slow count of 1-2-3-4 while deflating the lower abdomen.

11. Repeat steps 5 through 10 six times.

12. Relax for a few minutes before going on to Exercise 6.

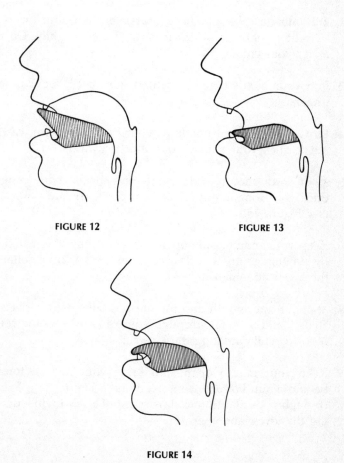

FIGURE 12   FIGURE 13

FIGURE 14

EXERCISE 6

Releasing Tension at the Root of the Tongue

During this exercise, be sure to hold your head erect; in stretching the tongue downward toward the chin, the head tends to dip, causing the under-chin and neck muscles to tighten.

When your tongue is stretched as far as possible toward your chin, as in step 5 below, be sure your mouth remains wide open.

1. Stand up straight with your feet 10 to 12 inches apart.

2. Tilt your head back as far as possible; then return it to an upright position in which it is tilted back slightly. Do not lower your chin.

3. Join your hands together behind your back, locking your fingers.

4. Lower your locked hands to your buttocks, being careful not to stick your tailbone out and backward.

5. Open your mouth wide, stretching the jawbone hinges. Stick your tongue out as far as possible toward your chin (see Figure 15).

6. Keep your mouth wide open and your tongue out. Exhale by blowing gently to a slow count of 1-2-3-4 while deflating the lower abdomen.

7. Maintain the mouth and tongue positions as described in steps 5 and 6. Inhale through your mouth to a slow count of 1-2-3 while inflating the lower abdomen.

8. Keep your mouth open, and bring your relaxed tongue behind your bottom front teeth (see Figure 16). Exhale through your mouth to a slow count of 1-2-3-4 while deflating the lower abdomen.

9. Maintain the mouth and tongue positions described in step 8. Inhale through your mouth to a slow count of 1-2-3 while inflating the lower abdomen.

10. Repeat steps 5 through 9 five times.

11. Relax for a few minutes before going on to Exercise 7.

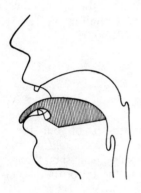

FIGURE 15

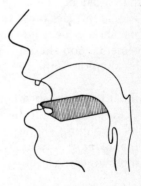

FIGURE 16

EXERCISE 7

Activating the Tongue Muscles

In this exercise, the syllable *toh* is a nonvocal or aspirated sound, as in whispering, made merely by the quick release of breath. It sounds like *tore* without the *r* sound, except that it is produced without the involvement of the voice box. Air should explode out between the front teeth and the tip of the tongue to produce a nonvocal outburst.

When making a double *toh-toh* sound, you should produce two explosive snapping sounds, one after the other, using only the lower abdominal muscles and inhaling no additional breath.

IMAGERY DRILL

Cannonball

Imagine an unobstructed channel from the pit of your stomach to the tip of your tongue as you produce nonvocal *tohs*. It may also help to imagine the *tohs* as cannonballs being shot through the channel from the pit of the stomach to the tip of the tongue and beyond.

In the exercise that follows, all snapping inward (rapid deflating) must be done with the lower abdominal and lower back torso muscles only. The only upper torso and chest movements should be slight natural reactions to the abdominal movements. You should experience no upward thrusts or jerks of the shoulders, the top back torso, or the chest.

1. Sit up straight in a chair with your head facing forward. Place both feet on the floor 6 to 8 inches apart, with your toes pointing slightly outward. Place your hands against the lower abdominal wall, palms inward and fingertips almost touching.

2. Place the tip of your tongue against the back of your bottom front teeth. Exhale through your mouth by blowing gently through slightly pursed lips to a slow count of 1-2-3-4-5-6 while deflating the lower abdominal wall, using your fingertips to apply extra pressure.

3. Place the tip of your tongue firmly against your top front teeth. With your mouth closed, inhale through your nose to a slow count of 1-2-3-4-5 while inflating the lower abdominal wall.

4. Bring the tip of your tongue between your top and bottom front teeth. Release the syllable *toh* explosively, dropping your jaw as you do so (see Figure 17). Do not retract your tongue toward your throat but simply release the tip of your tongue from your front teeth while dropping your jaw. Simultaneously snap the lower abdominal wall inward, assisting with pressure from your fingertips.

5. Exhale the remaining air.

6. Repeat steps 3 through 5 ten times.

7. Relax, and rest for a moment.

8. Repeat steps 3 through 6 again, substituting a double *toh-toh* sound (staccato) for *toh*.

9. Repeat step 8 ten times.

10. Relax, and rest briefly.

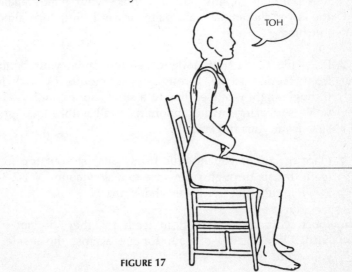

FIGURE 17

EXERCISE 8

Control of the Tip and the Root of the Tongue

The purpose of this exercise is to create awareness of core energy. The sound *tse* is a nonvocalized tight hissing sound produced by a continuous stream of breath. To make the *tse* sound, bring your top and bottom teeth together, but do not bite down hard. Place the tip of your tongue gently against the back of your front teeth. It's important for the tongue not to press too strongly against the front teeth, as extreme pressure causes tension in the neck and tongue. Exhale in an even, steady, unrushed stream of breath to produce not a *se* but a *tse* sound.

Although pressure is being produced by a continuous deflation of the lower abdominal wall, this deflation should not be overly exaggerated with too much inward motion of the abdominal wall. You can avoid this tendency by creating an imaginary counterforce from within, such as an expanding sensation within your lower abdomen as you deflate it. In this way, a much more controlled pressure of the abdominal wall can be produced and put to use.

1. Sit up straight in a chair with your head tilted back slightly. Place your feet on the floor 6 to 8 inches apart, with your toes pointing slightly outward. Place your hands against the lower abdominal wall, palms inward, fingertips almost touching.

2. Place the tip of your tongue gently against your bottom front teeth. Exhale through your mouth by blowing through slightly pursed lips to a slow count of 1-2-3-4-5-6, while squeezing in the abdominal wall with added pressure from your fingertips.

3. Place the tip of your tongue firmly against your top front teeth. Inhale through your nose to a slow count of 1-2-3-4-5, while inflating the lower abdomen.

4. Touch your top and bottom teeth together; do not bite hard. Place the tip of your tongue against the inside of your front teeth.

5. Exhale by producing a sustained *tse* sound (see Figure 18) while performing the following steps alternately:

   □ Roll your head in a clockwise circle once, then counter-clockwise once.

   □ Seesaw your shoulders up and down twice.

6. As you maintain the sustained *tse* sound, you will begin to feel a gradual tightening of a central spot in the depth of the lower abdomen. You are beginning to localize and gain an awareness of your core. Continue making the sustained *tse* sound until your breath is depleted.

7. Hold the deflated position for a few seconds. Then give an extra squeeze of the abdominal muscles, with added pressure from your fingertips, to expel any remaining air with an additional *tse*.

8. Immediately inhale deeply through your nose, with the tip of your tongue firmly against your top front teeth. Settle your breath, and hold it for a few seconds.

9. Exhale and relax for a minute or two. Repeat steps 2 through 8 three times, resting between each repetition.

10. Relax, and rest briefly.

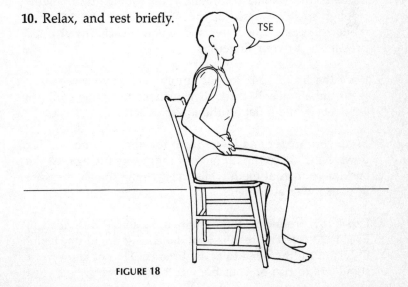

FIGURE 18

EXERCISE 9

Further Control of the Tongue

The purpose of this exercise is to learn how to maintain constant control of the core while sitting, standing, walking, running, jumping, or performing other movements.

When rising from a sitting to a standing position in step 6, take care not to shift pressure away from the core, the center of the lower abdomen.

In step 7, be especially careful not to let the center point shift to the chest, shoulders, or neck. Steady fingertip pressure on the lower abdomen will help alleviate this tendency to shift.

1. Sit up straight in a chair facing a desk or table. Place your feet on the floor with your weight on your toes, as if you were about to stand up. Place one foot slightly in front of the other.

2. Place your right hand (or your left, if you are left-handed) on the table top, palm down. Place the other hand against the lower abdominal wall, palm inward.

3. Place the tip of your tongue lightly against your bottom front teeth. Exhale through your mouth by blowing through slightly pursed lips to a slow count of 1-2-3-4-5-6, while squeezing the lower abdominal muscle inward and pressing with your fingertips.

4. Place the tip of your tongue firmly against your top front teeth. Inhale deeply through your nose to a slow count of 1-2-3-4-5, while inflating the lower abdomen.

5. Bring your upper and lower teeth together, but do not bite down hard. Place the tip of your tongue gently against the back of your front teeth while maintaining the air pressure in your lower abdomen.

6. Exhale by producing the sustained *tse* sound described in Exercise 8 (see Figure 19). Simultaneously, stand up, using the hand on the table to assist balance. Do not allow your shoulders to rise or your body to bend forward.

7. When you have reached an upright position, continue the *tse* sound evenly and firmly, using your lower abdominal and lower back muscles to maintain breath support (see Figure 20).

8. When your breath is depleted, hold in that state for 2 to 3 seconds. Then blow out forcefully, deflating the abdominal wall to expel any remaining air.

9. Immediately inhale deeply through your nose with the tip of your tongue held firmly against your top front teeth. Hold your breath without straining for a few seconds.

10. Slowly and deeply exhale and inhale three times, with accompanying lower abdomen deflation and inflation.

11. Relax, and rest for a moment.

12. Repeat this exercise three times with a rest interval between repetitions.

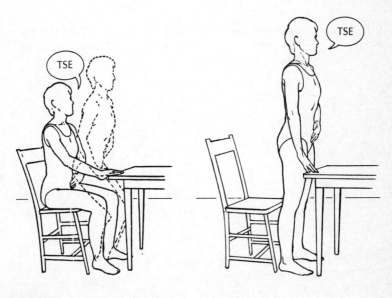

FIGURE 19   **FIGURE 20**

EXERCISE 10

Spreading the Breath to the Base of the Torso

A cross-legged sitting position induces maximum awareness of the lower torso base as a result of the tension that is concentrated there. The tension is produced by assembling the torso weight and the weight of the four limbs at a single pivot platform that supports the entire body. Many people are unaccustomed to the cross-legged position; its awkwardness and discomfort make them more aware of that area.

When you are sitting in the cross-legged position, your shoulders may tense up. By resting your elbows on bent knees, you can thwart that tendency and keep the weight focused downward. In this position, whether you are inhaling or exhaling, imagine yourself as a pyramid that is stable and firmly anchored.

If you find it difficult or uncomfortable to sit cross-legged on the floor, you may sit on one or more firm cushions or on a low stool with your legs crossed in front. Place your hands palm down on your knees or in your lap with your fingers pointing inward.

1. Sit up straight in a cross-legged position. Bend your arms, resting your elbows on your knees. Join your hands by interlocking your fingers (see Figure 21).

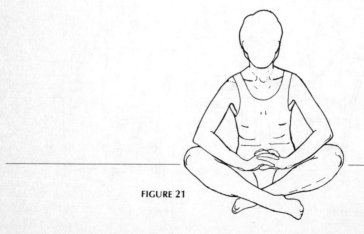

FIGURE 21

2. Place the tip of your tongue against your bottom front teeth. Exhale through your nose to a slow count of 1-2-3-4, while deflating the lower abdominal wall.

3. Place the tip of your tongue against your top front teeth. Inhale through your nose to a slow count of 1-2-3-4-5, while bending forward gradually as far as possible, directing your head toward the floor, and inflating your lower back torso. Let your elbows and lower arms press on your knees to assist in lowering your knees toward the floor (see Figure 22). (If you are sitting in an elevated position on a cushion or stool, let your elbows and arms spread out and forward.)

4. Place the tip of your tongue against your bottom front teeth. Exhale through your mouth to a slow count of 1-2-3-4, while slowly returning to your original position and relaxing the elbow pressure on your knees. Do not deflate the lower abdominal wall; let the lower back wall react naturally to the sitting up motion.

5. Repeat steps 3 and 4 five times.

6. Lie down on your back, legs extended in front. Relax.

FIGURE 22

EXERCISE 11

Stretching and Expanding the Side Muscles of the Lower Torso

Raising your hands above your head stretches the torso lengthwise. The previous exercises should have stretched your lower torso sideways sufficiently to enable you to maintain a stable, anchored base during this exercise.

In a left-right, backward-forward sequence of movements while inhaling and exhaling, you will learn to squeeze air out of your torso one side at a time, and then draw air back into your torso one side at a time. This action will allow you to make each repeated inhalation and exhalation more emphatic.

1. Stand up straight with your feet spread apart to the width of your shoulders. Point your toes slightly outward.

2. Raise your arms over your head and lock your fingers, palms down, to form an arch (see Figure 23).

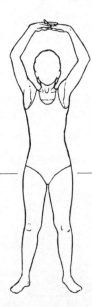

FIGURE 23

3. Place the tip of your tongue lightly against your bottom front teeth. Exhale through your mouth by blowing gently through slightly pursed lips to a slow count of 1-2-3-4-5-6. Simultaneously:

   ☐ Rock the arch from the waist, left-right-left-right on the counts 1-2-3-4, and slowly deflate the lower abdomen (see Figures 24 and 25).

   ☐ Return on counts 5 and 6 to the center upright position described in step 2.

4. Place the tip of your tongue firmly against your top front teeth. Inhale deeply through your nose to a slow count of 1-2-3-4-5. Simultaneously:

   ☐ Bend in an arch from the waist, moving forward-backward-forward-backward to a slow count of 1-2-3-4, and inflate the lower back and abdomen (see Figures 26 and 27).

   ☐ Return to the center upright position on count 5 (see Figure 23).

5. Repeat steps 3 and 4 six times.

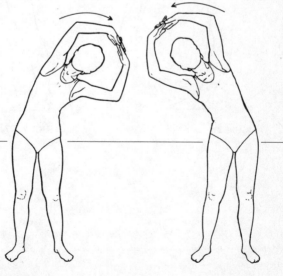

FIGURE 24   FIGURE 25

6. Exhale through your mouth to a slow count of 1-2-3-4-5-6-7-8, while deflating the lower abdomen and lowering your arms to your sides.

7. Inhale, relax, and rest for a moment.

8. Repeat this exercise three more times with a rest between each repetition.

9. Relax, and rest.

FIGURE 26   FIGURE 27

Thoughts on Lesson 2

By this time, your muscles should be growing more sensitive and responsive, and your awareness of the core gradually becoming more acute.

Exercises 1 through 11 were geared toward maximum inflation and deflation of the abdomen. Keeping in mind the image of the body as a pyramid, you should begin to cultivate a sensation of physical stability.

Controlling the Breath

In addition to the tongue, the neck is another part of the body that must be fully relaxed before effective breathing can take place. Without some form of abdominal breathing, however, it is difficult to relax the neck. To break this circle, you must follow a regimen that focuses alternately on developing each of these skills so that they reinforce each other.

It is not easy to get rid of unwanted tension in the neck, tongue, or shoulders. Tension in these areas must be relocated to a place where, properly handled, it can be recycled into useful energy. The core is such a place. Awareness of the core must be established before harmful tensions can be effectively eliminated. This lesson also reestablishes the relationship between the tongue and the core by reviewing Exercise 7.

From now on, you will no longer be instructed to rest between exercises. Let your physical condition determine when you need to rest, and for how long.

The Elastic Band Imagery Drill will help you to relax your neck as well as your chest and back muscles. You will feel taller, straighter, and free of muscle tension, especially in the neck area.

IMAGERY DRILL

Elastic Band

Visualize your spine, with its ability to bend in any direction. Imagine one elastic band attached from your chin to your lower abdomen, and another attached from the back of your head (at the top) to your lower back. Bend backward, with your chin lifted high, and feel the front elastic band stretching to its utmost. Bend forward with your head dipping low and feel the back elastic band stretching as much as possible.

Imagine that these elastic bands are too stiff and tight. As you bend backward and forward you lengthen the bands and relax the stiffness and tightness.

EXERCISE 12

Directing the Breath to the Lower Abdomen

Lying down should be a very relaxed position, yet many people find themselves unable to relax sufficiently to fall asleep. To do away with unwanted tension, focus your mind on the core by directing the breath there. This will create a magnetic center where tensions can be gathered and dispelled or recycled. In this exercise, tension is maintained at the core and used to bend the knees and pull the feet toward the body. Drawing the knees to the chest further emphasizes the involvement of the lower back in abdominal breathing.

1. Lie on the floor or bed with your feet together. Place your hands, palms down, on the floor by your sides, 12 to 14 inches away from the body (see Figure 28).

2. Bend your knees and slide your feet flat along the floor until they are as close to your body as possible (see Figure 29).

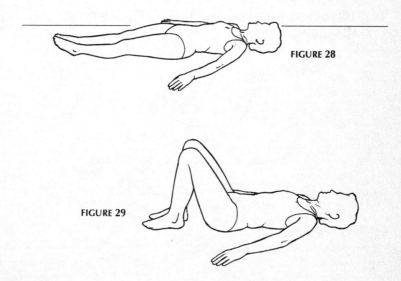

FIGURE 28

FIGURE 29

3. Place the tip of your tongue against your bottom front teeth. Exhale on the counts of 1 and 2 by blowing through your mouth in two strong gusts (one gust to each count), while deflating the lower abdomen and doing the following steps:

   □ With the first gust, swing your knees up as close to your chest as possible, lifting your feet off the floor (see Figure 30).

   □ With the second gust, return your feet to the floor (see Figure 29).

4. Place the tip of your tongue against your top front teeth. Inhale through your nose in two strong sniffs (one to each count), while inflating the lower abdomen and doing the following steps:

   □ With the first sniff, swing your knees up as close to your chest as possible, lifting your feet off the floor (see Figure 30).

   □ With the second sniff, return your feet to the floor (see Figure 29).

5. Repeat steps 3 and 4 in a rocking motion ten times.

6. Exhale as you straighten your legs, and return to your original position.

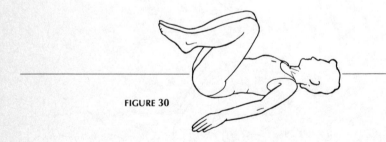

FIGURE 30

EXERCISE 13

Directing the Breath to the Lower Back

This exercise is intended to stretch the spine, back muscles, and tendons at the same time that breathing is being controlled. When you hook your arms under your knees, as in step 3, you stretch the back and side muscles outward and keep your shoulders from heaving. Bending your head and touching your face to your knees extends your back and the back of your neck lengthwise.

In the ball position, with your stomach curled inside, exhaling further shrinks the front abdominal wall. In this position, the back is extended and the front is contracted as much as possible. This position also directs the maximum amount of breath to the lower back while restricting intake to the front. Extreme positions such as this one help you develop agility.

1. Sit up straight on the floor and stretch your legs out in front of you. Place your feet together and point your toes, making sure you are sitting up straight. Hold your head in an upright position, being careful not to drop your chin. Place your hands on your knees, palms down (see Figure 31).

2. Slide your feet toward you, bending your knees (see Figure 32).

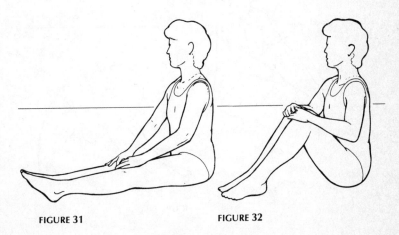

FIGURE 31   FIGURE 32

3. Hook your arms under your knees by reaching under the knees with your right hand to hold your left elbow or near to it, and with your left hand to hold your right elbow or near to it (see Figure 33).

4. Bend your head over and touch your face to your knees, or as close as you can comfortably manage (see Figure 34).

5. Place the tip of your tongue against your bottom front teeth. Exhale through your mouth by blowing gently through slightly pursed lips to a slow count of 1-2-3-4-5-6-7-8, while completely deflating the lower abdomen.

6. Hold your breath and remain still for a few seconds.

7. Place the tip of your tongue against your top front teeth. Inhale through your nose to a slow count of 1-2-3-4-5-6-7, while inflating the lower abdomen. As you inhale, think of your lower torso as a round balloon that inflates as you

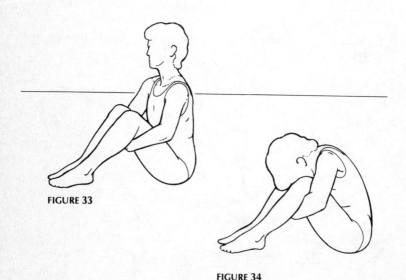

FIGURE 33

FIGURE 34

inhale steadily to the count of 1-2-3-4-5. On the last two counts, make an extra effort to fully inflate the balloon, using your lower back and side muscles.

8. Repeat steps 5 through 7 five times.

9. Slowly let go of all muscle tension, stretching your legs forward and straightening your neck and body.

10. Stand up slowly. Stretch your body, arms, and legs. Loosen all your joints. Roll your head clockwise and counter-clockwise several times. Then relax and allow your arms to dangle.

REVIEW   EXERCISES 7 AND 10 FROM LESSON 2

For the exercises that follow, you must be very aware of the relationship between your tongue and the act of breathing to and from the core. Reread the introductory material for Lesson 2 before reviewing Exercise 7.

A review of Exercise 10 gives you the opportunity to loosen the lower torso and establish a firmer focus on your core. This exercise will also loosen the muscles and tendons at the back of the neck in preparation for Exercises 14 and 15.

EXERCISE 14

Relieving Neck Tension

Sitting up straight with your feet as far apart as possible again focuses attention on the lower abdominal area, the core's cradle. Bending your knees with your feet far apart makes you more fully aware of the lower back. Placing your hands on your knees helps you maintain your balance, and lowers and relaxes the shoulders and upper chest muscles as well. Be sure that your shoulders remain relaxed as you bend your knees and shift your hands from knees to ankles.

By rolling your head in a dangling, relaxed position, you ensure that the neck is completely relaxed while the lower torso is energetically controlling the breathing.

1. Sit up straight on the floor with your legs spread as far apart as is comfortably possible. Place your hands on your knees, palms down (see Figure 35).

2. Bend your knees to an angle of approximately 120 degrees by sliding your feet along the floor toward you. Keep your feet far apart, and point your toes outward (see Figure 36).

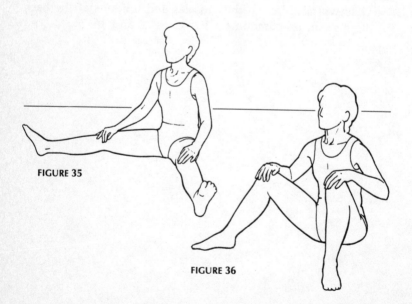

FIGURE 35

FIGURE 36

3. Bend your body forward. Stretch your arms along and over your legs, and gently grasp your ankles (or your legs as near your ankles as possible) with your hands. Spread your elbows out and forward.

4. Let your head dangle toward the floor.

5. Place the tip of your tongue against your bottom front teeth. Exhale through your mouth by blowing gently through slightly pursed lips to a slow count of 1-2-3-4-5-6-7 in the following manner:

   □ Roll your head to the right twice in big circles on counts 1 and 2.

   □ Dangle your head forward toward the floor on count 3.

   □ Roll your head to the left twice in big circles on counts 4 and 5.

   □ Dangle your head forward toward the floor on counts 6 and 7.

   All these movements are performed as you slowly deflate the lower abdominal and lower back walls (see Figure 37).

6. Place the tip of your tongue against your top front teeth. Inhale through your nose to a slow count of 1-2-3-4-5-6-7, going through the head-rotation-and-dangling sequence described in step 5, while inflating the lower abdomen and the lower back.

7. Repeat steps 5 and 6 three times.

8. Straighten your legs, lie on the floor, and relax.

FIGURE 37

EXERCISE 15

Relieving Shoulder Tension

Swinging your arms relaxes your shoulders and loosens the base of the neck. Your arms should dangle and swing freely. It is preferable to keep your elbow joints loose by letting your elbows bend slightly, as is their natural tendency.

Your neck muscles should not be tense during the alternating neck stretches. Relax!

1. Stand up straight with your feet 12 to 14 inches apart and your toes pointed slightly outward.

2. Lower your shoulders, and loosen your shoulder joints. Let your arms and hands dangle at your sides (see Figure 38). Stretch and extend your neck upward.

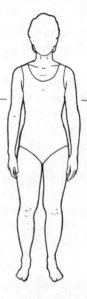

FIGURE 38

3. Place the tip of your tongue against your bottom front teeth. Gently tilt your head back as far as possible to stretch the front of your neck. Exhale through your mouth by blowing vigorously through slightly pursed lips to a slow count of 1-2, while deflating the lower abdomen and doing the following:

☐ On the first count, swing your arms to the left, bringing your hands toward waist level (see Figure 39).

☐ On the second count, swing your arms to the right, bringing your hands toward waist level (see Figure 40).

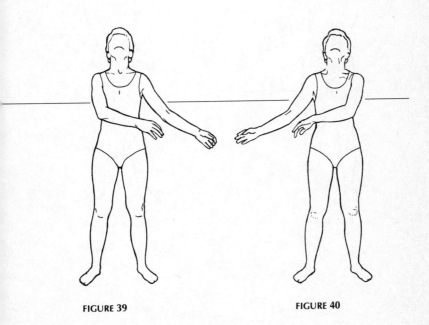

FIGURE 39   FIGURE 40

4. Place the tip of your tongue against your top front teeth. Bend your head forward as far as possible to stretch the back of your neck. Inhale vigorously through your nose to a slow count of 1-2, while inflating the lower abdomen and doing the following:

☐ On the first count, swing your arms to the left, bringing your hands toward waist level (see Figure 41).

☐ On the second count, swing your arms to the right, bringing your hands toward waist level (see Figure 42).

5. Repeat steps 3 and 4 nine times.

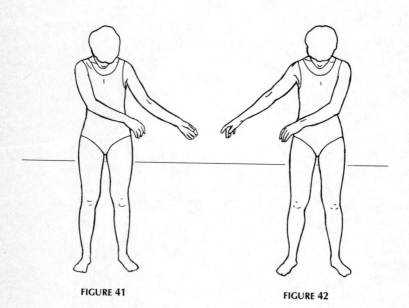

FIGURE 41   FIGURE 42

EXERCISE 16

Stretching the Chest Muscles

Swinging your arms forward and backward as suggested in this exercise further relaxes the front and back of the rib cage.

1. Stand up straight with your feet 10 to 12 inches apart and your toes turned slightly outward.

2. Lower your shoulders, and loosen your shoulder joints. Let your arms and hands dangle at your sides. Stretch and extend your neck.

3. Place the tip of your tongue against your bottom front teeth. Tilt your head back as far as possible to stretch the front of your neck. Exhale through your mouth by blowing

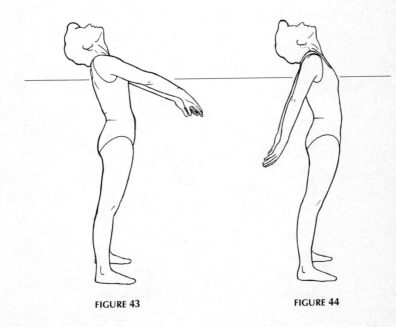

FIGURE 43   FIGURE 44

vigorously through slightly pursed lips to a slow count of 1-2, while deflating the lower abdomen and doing the following:

☐ On the first count, swing your arms forward, bringing your hands toward shoulder height (see Figure 43).

☐ On the second count, keeping your head back, swing your arms back as far as possible (see Figure 44).

4. Place the tip of your tongue against your top front teeth. Bend your head forward as far as possible to stretch the back of your neck. Inhale intensely through your nose to a slow count of 1-2, while inflating the lower abdomen and doing the following:

☐ On the first count, swing your arms forward toward shoulder level (see Figure 45).

☐ On the second count, keeping your head back, swing your arms back as far as possible (see Figure 46).

5. Repeat steps 3 and 4 nine times.

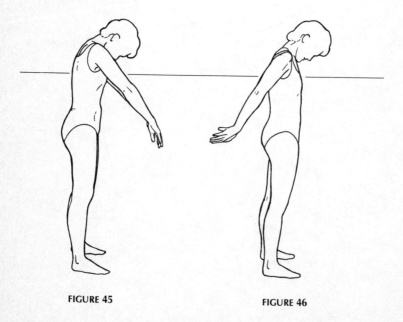

FIGURE 45   **FIGURE 46**

EXERCISE 17

Leading the Breath to the Core

This long, detailed exercise is divided into two sections. Steps 1 through 7 aim to reveal more completely the location of the core and its cradle through a back-arching movement that induces the lower abdominal wall to stretch as it deflates during exhalation. This movement establishes a strong awareness of the core. After the lower abdomen is completely deflated, you will forcefully expand it, drawing a big gulp of air into the core and its surrounding area. Steps 8 through 10 take advantage of techniques learned in Lesson 1 by repeating deep breathing in a relaxed standing position. Read through the instructions several times so that you understand the steps and will be able to perform the exercise comfortably and easily.

1. Stand up straight with your feet 12 to 14 inches apart and your toes pointed slightly outward. Place your hands on the lower abdominal wall, palms inward, fingers almost touching (see Figure 47).

FIGURE 47

2. Place the tip of your tongue against your bottom front teeth. Exhale through your mouth by blowing gently through slightly pursed lips to a slow count of 1-2-3-4-5-6-7-8-9-10-11-12, while gradually deflating the lower abdomen and giving it a big squeeze inward as your breath is depleted.

3. As you hold this deflated state, bend your head back with your chin upward (see Figure 48). Steps 3 through 5 should take only a few seconds, so no inhalation is necessary.

4. Bring your arms behind your back, joining your hands by interlocking the fingers. Rest your joined hands on your buttocks (see Figure 49.)

5. Arch back gradually while pushing your locked hands downward and tilting your chin high with your mouth closed. Be sure not to bend your knees (see Figure 50). As you continue to arch back in this manner, you will feel a very strong sensation in the lower abdomen.

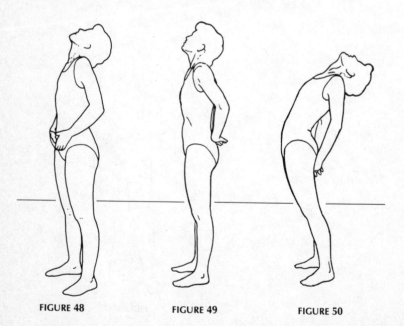

FIGURE 48   FIGURE 49   FIGURE 50

6. Give a strong squeeze inward with the lower abdominal muscles to expel the last traces of breath.

7. Immediately relax your tongue, resting it against your bottom front teeth, and inhale through your mouth, completely filling the core cradle (lower abdomen). Hold your breath for a few seconds, letting it sink deeply into the core and stabilize and anchor there.

As you continue with the second part of Exercise 17, do not attempt, in step 8, to squeeze out air excessively. This excessive effort might shift the pivot point upward to the chest, completely undoing your accomplishment of locating the core in order to anchor the breath there.

8. Loosen all muscle tension. Slowly return to a normal standing position, letting your arms and hands dangle at your sides. Place the tip of your tongue against your bottom front teeth. Exhale slowly through your mouth, maintaining the sensation of being anchored. Stop the exhalation when your breath seems completely expelled from the lower abdomen.

9. Place the tip of your relaxed tongue against your slightly parted top and bottom front teeth. Inhale slowly and deeply through your nose, while inflating the lower abdomen. Continue to hold the tip of your tongue at the same position. Exhale slowly and deeply through your nose while deflating the lower abdomen.

10. Repeat step 9 five times.

11. Relax, and rest.

12. Repeat this exercise, steps 1 through 11, three or four times. Rest between each repetition.

Thoughts on Lesson 3

Having completed Lesson 3, you should now be able to apply the abdominal deep-breathing technique to improve your daily breathing. Use the tongue position described in step 9 of Exercise 17 in your everyday breathing. For instance, as you watch TV, walk, exercise, or just relax, inflate and deflate your lower abdomen. Remember, inflate for inhalation and deflate for exhalation. The more you practice this technique, the more habitual it will become.

Since deep breathing stimulates and strengthens the core, it is advisable to do it as frequently as you can. At this stage, you should be able to sense the location of the core without great effort. Think frequently of its location, and familiarize yourself with its presence.

Varying and Extending the Breath

All of the exercises in this book are carefully planned to accomplish specific purposes. It is impossible to design special exercises or to plan special lessons to suit each individual's needs. You have now learned enough about *chi yi* to feel free to repeat those exercises that you find to be especially beneficial, even though they may not be included in a particular lesson. But be careful not to overexert yourself. Allow sufficient rest time between exercises. Always stop to rest if you become dizzy.

In Lesson 4 and later lessons, unless otherwise specified, the term *inhale* will always mean breathing in through the nose with the tip of the tongue against the top front teeth, and *exhale* will always mean blowing out gently through slightly pursed lips with the tip of the tongue placed lightly against the bottom front teeth.

Tongue positions for inhalation and exhalation may now be executed more casually, as long as the tongue remains flexible and unobtrusive and is not tense, retracted, or lumping. As you review Exercises 8 and 9 in this lesson, apply the following image.

IMAGERY DRILL

Kite

Imagine controlling your tongue the same way you would fly a kite. You control your kite from the end of the string that you hold in your hand. But to control it well, under conditions of varying wind direction and intensity, you must have great dexterity in your hand.

Likewise, the capability of your tongue relies a great deal on how well you can control it from the core. Imagine your tongue as the kite, and control it from your core, way down in the center of your lower abdomen. You will discover how well your tongue can perform and respond. Apply this image in this lesson as you review Exercises 8 and 9.

REVIEW EXERCISES 12 AND 13 FROM LESSON 3, AND
EXERCISES 8 AND 9 FROM LESSON 2

Lesson 4 begins with a review of anchoring the breath in four different positions: lying flat, sitting on the floor, sitting in a chair, and standing up. This review session is fairly strenuous. Be easy on yourself, and take a sufficient break before going on to Exercise 18. Repeat each of the review exercises as many times as necessary to feel you have mastered them thoroughly.

EXERCISE 18

Flexing the Muscles of the Lower Sides and Back

Like Exercise 12, Exercise 18 helps develop conscious control of a well-anchored breathing technique in a lying position. This exercise also develops the sides of the lower torso.

Practicing *chi yi* while lying in a twisted position will develop your ability to breathe properly in other twisted positions, whether sitting, standing, or moving.

1. Lie flat on your back with your feet 20 to 22 inches apart and your toes pointed. Your head should face the ceiling. Stretch your arms straight out to your sides, palms up (see Figure 51).

2. Exhale completely while deflating the abdomen.

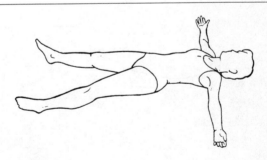

FIGURE 51

3. Inhale deeply while doing the following steps simultaneously (see Figure 52):

  □ Swing your right hand over in a semicircle and clap it to your left hand, turning your head toward the left.

  □ Inflate your abdomen, expanding the lower back and sides.

  □ Keep both heels stationary on the floor.

4. Exhale completely while doing the following steps simultaneously:

  □ Swing your right hand back over to the floor to its original position.

  □ Turn your head back to its original position (see Figure 51).

  □ Deflate your lower abdomen.

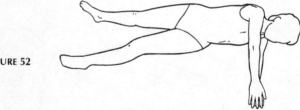

FIGURE 52

5. Inhale deeply while doing the following steps simultaneously (see Figure 53):

   □ Swing your left hand over in a semicircle and clap it to your right hand, turning your head toward the right.

   □ Inflate your abdomen, expanding the lower back and sides.

   □ Keep both your heels stationary on the floor.

6. Exhale completely while doing the following steps simultaneously:

   □ Swing your left hand back over to the floor to its original position (see Figure 51).

   □ Turn your head back to its original position facing the ceiling.

   □ Deflate your lower abdomen.

7. Repeat steps 3 through 6 five times.

8. Lie stretched out on floor, and relax.

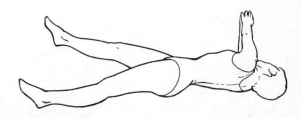

FIGURE 53

EXERCISE 19

Flexing the Lower Abdominal Muscles

In this doubled-up position, the tendons and muscles of the feet and legs are thoroughly stretched. This stretched sensation is passed on up to the base of the torso (the lower abdomen). In bending over, you further extend this sensation up your back to your neck and even to the top of your head. Your entire body is in a state of attention. Centralize all your attention at the core. Focusing in this way will induce your breathing to come and go from the core.

Exhaling while bending over squeezes air out of the abdomen. When you inhale as you sit up, air is drawn easily into the abdomen.

1. Kneel on the floor with your knees together; keep your back straight and sit on your heels. Place your hands in your lap, palms down, fingers pointing forward, and thumbs inward. Keep your elbows by your sides. Lower and relax your shoulders. Hold your head up straight, being careful not to lower your chin (see Figure 54). (If you find it difficult to sit on your heels, place a pillow or cushion on your heels and sit on that.)

FIGURE 54   FIGURE 55

2. Exhale to a slow count of 1-2-3-4-5-6-7-8-9-10, while doing the following steps simultaneously (see Figure 55):

   □ Bend forward from the hips, and curve your back.

   □ Bring your forehead slowly to the floor, or as low as possible.

3. Inhale rapidly to a slow count of 1-2-3, while doing the following steps simultaneously:

   □ Straighten up, returning to your original kneeling position (see Figure 56).

   □ Expand your lower abdomen and sides. Do not lift your shoulders or raise your chest. Straighten your neck and lift your head slightly.

4. Repeat steps 2 and 3 five times.

5. Sit up, breathe normally, and relax for a moment.

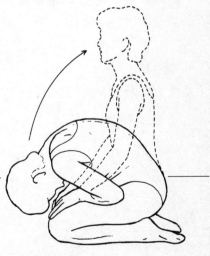

FIGURE 56

EXERCISE 20

Flexing the Lower Back Muscles

This exercise promotes inflation of the lower back torso. Exhaling while deflating all sides of the lower torso in an upright sitting position prepares you for your next inhalation. As you bend over while inhaling, the air you take in will significantly fill up the lower back as the front abdomen is being depressed.

1. Kneel on the floor with your knees together; keep your back straight and sit on your heels. Place your hands in your lap, palms down, fingers pointing forward, and thumbs inward. Keep your elbows at your sides. Lower and relax your shoulders. Hold your head up straight, being careful not to lower your chin (see Figure 57).

2. Exhale to a slow count of 1-2-3-4-5-6-7-8-9-10-11-12, while deflating the lower abdomen.

3. Inhale to a slow count of 1-2-3, while doing the following steps simultaneously (see Figure 58):

   ☐ Bend forward from the hips, bringing your forehead to the floor, or as low as possible.

   ☐ Inflate the lower back and sides.

FIGURE 57   FIGURE 58

4. Exhale to a slow count of 1-2-3-4-5-6-7-8-9-10, while doing the following steps simultaneously:

    ☐ Straighten up, returning to your original kneeling position (see Figure 59).

    ☐ Deflate the lower abdomen, back, and sides.

5. Repeat steps 3 and 4 five times.

6. Inhale, and return to the original step 1 position.

7. Exhale and relax.

Note: To help you visualize the deep breathing that involves inflating and deflating of the lower front, the lower back, and the lower sides simultaneously, from now on these areas will be called the *lower circumference* when spoken of as a unit.

REVIEW   EXERCISES 14, 15, AND 16 FROM LESSON 3

In preparation for Exercises 21 and 22, this review of Exercises 14, 15, and 16 serves primarily as a reminder of how to relax your neck and shoulders without losing your awareness of the core, the focal point of the flow of breath.

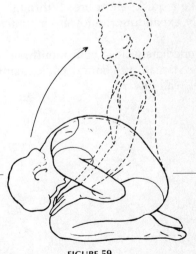

FIGURE 59

EXERCISE 21

Developing Agility of the Abdominal and Lower Back Muscles

After completing the neck-shoulder-upper torso relaxation exercises, you should now be ready to add movements that will relax the tongue as well.

Without tension in the neck, shoulders, and upper torso, tongue movement will automatically be controlled by the tongue's roots at the core.

Both the *toh* and *pah* are nonvocal, aspirated, exploding sounds.

1. Stand up straight with your feet 10 to 12 inches apart and your toes pointed slightly out.

2. Place your hands against the lower abdominal wall, palms inward, fingers almost touching, to monitor abdominal wall movements.

3. Place the tip of your tongue firmly against your top front teeth. Make an explosive staccato *toh* sound, while snapping the lower abdominal wall inward (see Figure 60).

4. Take a quick, short breath through your mouth, while rapidly expanding the lower circumference.

5. Immediately close your mouth, and follow with an exploding staccato *pah* sound while snapping the lower abdominal wall inward.

Note: Do not retract your tongue into the back of the mouth cavity when exploding the *toh* or *pah*. Drop your jaw to assist the rapid opening of the mouth for exploding sounds.

6. Repeat steps 3 through 5 ten times.

7. Take a slow, deep breath, exhale and relax.

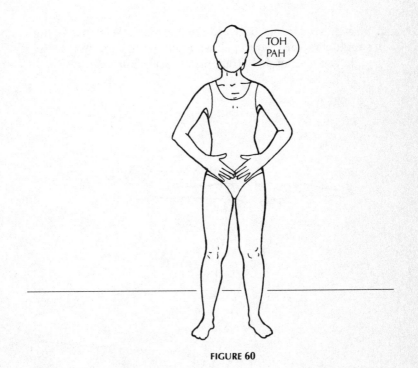

FIGURE 60

EXERCISE 22

Expanding the Base of the Torso

Now that your lower torso's agility is well developed by the previous exercises, let your upper torso be consciously involved in the breathing process, taking care to maintain your attention and weight consistently in the lower torso. The top and bottom parts of the torso must be very carefully balanced to avoid a tendency toward top-heaviness.

Spreading your arms expands the torso top. Keeping your feet wide apart while bending and unbending the knees prevents loss of awareness of the core.

1. Stand up straight with your feet spread apart a few inches wider than shoulder width. Point your toes slightly outward.

2. Stretch your arms outward to the sides, level with your shoulders. Turn your palms down with your fingers together and extended straight out (see Figure 61).

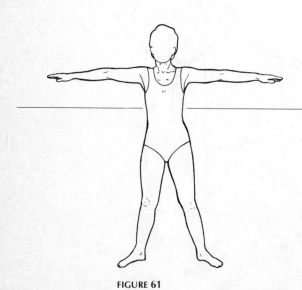

FIGURE 61

3. Inhale rapidly to a slow count of 1-2 and do the following steps simultaneously:

   ☐ Bend your knees outward over your toes (see Figure 62).

   ☐ Keep your elbows stationary and level with your shoulders, and swing your forearms in toward your collarbone. Join your fingertips; your fingers should meet a few inches below your chin.

   ☐ Keep your torso straight; do not allow your buttocks to stick out.

4. Exhale rapidly to a slow count of 1-2, deflating the abdomen and returning to your starting position, standing straight with arms outstretched and pointing out to opposite sides (see Figure 61).

5. Repeat steps 3 and 4 ten times.

6. Repeat step 3, and hold for 5 seconds.

7. Straighten your legs and let your arms dangle at your sides. Exhale slowly, deflate the abdomen, and relax.

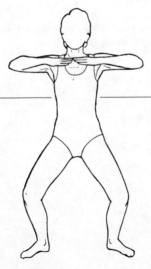

FIGURE 62

Thoughts on Lesson 4

The exercises in this lesson emphasize the lower sides of the torso (the lower waist) by inducing air to these areas with appropriate postures and movements. With your lower abdomen and lower back deflatable and inflatable, your sides should now also be as flexible. Your lower torso is now expandable in four dimensions, forming the lower circumference.

The lower circumference, together with your torso base, envelops the cradle of the core. External stimulation by the lower circumference activates your core to radiate inner energy throughout your entire being.

Throughout this book, we have often used vivid mental pictures to help you visualize how your body functions. If a certain mental image works for you, use it whenever you wish to overcome difficulties. If the following Coil of Rope Imagery Drill, or any other, helps you with your exercises, use it frequently until the effect wears off, and then substitute or invent another one.

IMAGERY DRILL

Coil of Rope

Imagine air entering and leaving your abdomen as a coil of rope with the bottom circle always remaining at the core.

LESSON FIVE

Using the Breath to Develop the Core

This lesson contains more review exercises than any previous lesson. It is important, at this advanced stage, to take the time to reexamine how each of these exercises induces the manner of breathing we seek. A thorough understanding of how certain movements and positions help induce specific breathing mechanisms will build confidence for improvisation in the future.

This lesson is the longest in the book; the repetitions indicated at the end of each exercise may be reduced in number. If you lack time or energy, it is better to cut down the number of repetitions in the review exercises than to skip any exercise entirely, since the order of the exercises—including the reviews—is designed to lead smoothly and effectively from one to the next.

REVIEW   EXERCISES 18, 19, AND 20 FROM LESSON 4

Review Exercises 18, 19, and 20, repeating each one as many times as necessary to accomplish their objectives effectively. You should now be able to perform these exercises more efficiently and meaningfully than you did when they first appeared in the previous lesson.

EXERCISE 23

Further Expanding the Lower Circumference

The movements in this exercise are very simple. Their purpose is to practice control of the breath flow, extending exhalation time and shortening inhalation time. In speech and singing, we inhale rapidly and exhale slowly to enable the breath to be sustained through a phrase.

A slight dizziness may occur at step 7 if you stand upright too rapidly, or if you are unaccustomed to bending over. Relax, and the feeling will quickly pass.

As you stand and bend over as far as possible, the weight of the torso is borne at and suspended from the torso base. In this position, it is easy to breathe automatically to the core.

During this exercise, be sure to keep track of the pace of your breathing so that you can sustain your exhalation for an extended time.

1. Stand up straight with your feet 18 to 20 inches apart and your toes pointed slightly outward.

2. Place your hands at your waist with palms inward and thumbs pointed toward the back (see Figure 63).

FIGURE 63

3. Bend over from the hips as far as possible (see Figure 64).

4. Exhale to a slow count of 1-2-3-4-5-6-7-8-9-10-11-12, while gradually pulling the abdominal wall inward (deflating).

5. Inhale deeply and fully to a slow count of 1-2, while expanding the lower circumference.

6. Repeat steps 4 and 5 five times. Monitor inflation and deflation of your sides with your hands.

7. Hold your breath, and stand up slowly (see Figure 65).

8. Exhale slowly.

9. Take a deep breath, and hold it at the core for a few seconds.

10. Relax and return to normal breathing.

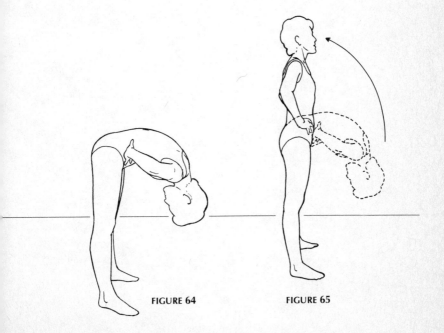

FIGURE 64   FIGURE 65

REVIEW EXERCISES 11, 8, AND 9 FROM LESSON 2,
AND EXERCISE 14 FROM LESSON 3

After practicing regulating your breath flow in Exercise 23, you should be able to perform Exercises 8 and 9 with much more understanding and skill. These two exercises can be made more beneficial by lengthening the *tse* sound by as many counts as possible. It will be interesting for you to test your own endurance.

Make sure that as you use your tongue to produce the *tse* sound you do not tighten your neck and shoulder muscles or unconsciously allow your anchored base (core) to rise. Keep that base low.

EXERCISE 24

Developing Core Sensation

This exercise focuses on a part of the anatomy that is seldom discussed in Western physical exercise programs. The rectal muscle is a sensitive part of the torso base. When this muscle is tightened at the same time as you swallow, you will feel a direct connection between the base of the core cradle and the opening of the throat. Combining this sensation with regulated exhalation creates an intense awareness of the core.

Pointing your toes downward and pushing your heels upward as indicated in step 5 of the following exercise will intensify the strength that emanates from the lower circumference.

Lowering your feet slowly to the floor as indicated in step 8 results in the greatest awareness of the core.

1. Lie flat on the floor. Place your hands by your sides, palms down, keeping your straightened legs together and pointing your toes (see Figure 66).

2. Inhale deeply and fully to a slow count of 1-2-3 while inflating the lower abdomen.

3. Hold your breath.

FIGURE 66

4. Keeping them together, lift both feet toward the ceiling. (If you have difficulty lifting your feet with your legs straight, bend your knees toward your chest and then straighten your legs upward as much as possible.)

5. Point your toes downward while pushing your heels upward (see Figure 67).

6. Tighten the rectal muscle.

7. Place the tip of your tongue firmly against your front teeth, and swallow.

8. Maintaining the position described in steps 4 through 6, exhale to a slow count of 1-2-3-4-5-6-7-8-9-10, while lowering your legs slowly to their original position on the floor (see Figure 68).

FIGURE 67

9. Inhale rapidly and deeply to a slow count of 1-2-3.

10. Remain lying down, and hold your breath for 3 seconds.

11. Exhale, and relax for a moment.

12. Repeat steps 2 through 11 two more times.

13. Sit up slowly. Bring your knees up to your chest.

14. Breathe deeply several times, and relax.

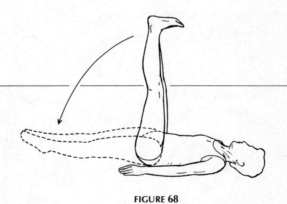

FIGURE 68

EXERCISE 25

Expanding and Stabilizing the Breath at the Core

Like Exercise 22, this exercise encourages the top, middle, and lower torso—including the entire length of the lungs—to be well-balanced and to function as a whole.

The arm movements help expand and relax the torso. Standing on tiptoe brings strength to the torso base.

1. Stand up straight with your feet 8 to 10 inches apart. Let your arms and hands dangle at your sides (see Figure 69).

2. Exhale completely to a slow count of 1-2-3-4-5-6-7-8-9-10, deflating the lower abdomen.

3. Inhale fully to a slow count of 1-2-3-4-5, inflating the lower circumference, while doing the following simultaneously (see Figure 70):

   □ Lift up your heels and stand on tiptoe.
   □ Raise your arms out to your sides
     at shoulder level.

FIGURE 69

4. Exhale completely to a slow count of 1-2-3-4-5-6, deflating the lower abdomen, while doing the following simultaneously:

   □ Lower your heels to the floor, and stand flat on your feet.

   □ Lower your arms to your sides.

5. Inhale fully to a slow count of 1-2-3-4-5, inflating the lower circumference and doing the following simultaneously (see Figure 71):

   □ Lift up your heels and stand on tiptoe.

   □ Raise your arms forward and upward toward the ceiling.

6. Exhale completely to a slow count of 1-2-3-4-5-6-7-8-9-10, deflating the lower abdomen, and doing the following simultaneously:

   □ Lower your heels to the floor, and stand flat on your feet.

   □ Lower your arms to your sides.

7. Repeat steps 3 through 6 eight times.

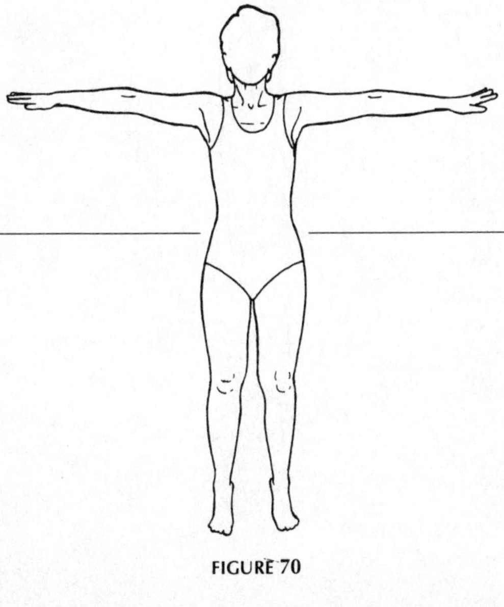

FIGURE 70 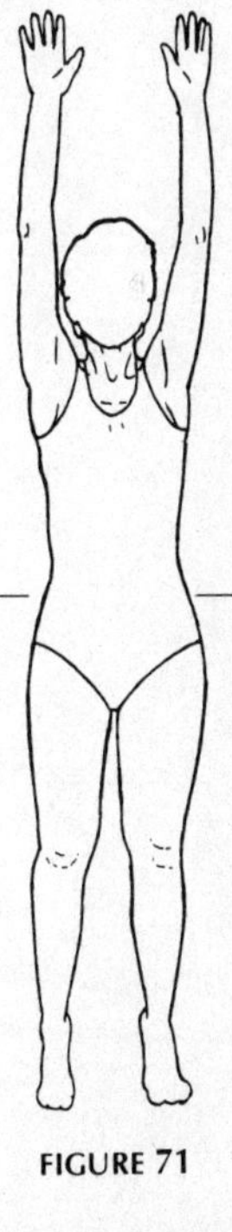   FIGURE 71

EXERCISE 26

Intensifying Core Sensation

This exercise puts the rectal muscle into action once more.

Tightening your fists in conjunction with contracting the rectal muscle focuses a pivotal energy at the core, spreading upward to the diaphragm.

When tightening your fists, take care not to tighten your shoulders and neck; in that area tension will obstruct air flow into the bottom of the lungs.

1. Stand up straight with your feet 12 to 14 inches apart. Let your arms dangle.

2. Exhale to a slow count of 1-2-3-4-5-6-7-8, doing the following steps simultaneously:

   □ Slowly bend forward at the hips as far as possible, keeping your knees straight (see Figure 72).

   □ Deflate the lower abdomen.

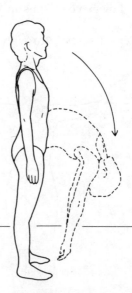

FIGURE 72

3. Holding the bent-over position, place your palms on your knees, fingers pointing inward. Bend your elbows and spread them outward (see Figure 73).

4. Inhale to a slow count of 1-2-3-4-5-6-7, doing the following steps simultaneously:

☐ Stand up slowly to an upright position.

☐ Raise your hands to head level, palms facing forward in front of your face, with your elbows still bent and spread.

5. Bring your palms to the sides of your head with your arms bent at right angles. Close your palms into tight fists (see Figure 74). Contract the rectal muscle, drawing it slightly upward.

FIGURE 74

FIGURE 73

6. Place the tip of your tongue against your top front teeth. Hold your head erect, tilting it back slightly. Swallow.

7. Immediately exhale as slowly as possible, doing the following steps simultaneously:

   □ Keep your fists tight, and gradually straighten your arms and lower your fists to your sides.

   □ Keep the rectal muscle contracted and drawn upward.

8. Continue exhaling slowly. You should be able to feel your core and all the muscles of your lower circumference tightening and exuding energy. Maintain muscle control until your breath is depleted.

9. Loosen your fists. Inhale and exhale deeply several times.

10. Repeat this exercise two more times, with a rest interval between repetitions.

Thoughts on the First Five Lessons

Having completed the first five lessons, you should have a clear inner vision of the location of the core, the primary objective of deep breathing. At this advanced stage of exercise, because of your increased awareness of disciplined breathing, you will no longer be given exact breath counts. Inhalation and exhalation can now be more relaxed and spontaneous. These less detailed directions will allow you greater flexibility and an opportunity to experiment sensibly and to adjust these exercises to fit your individual abilities.

You need no longer exaggerate abdominal inflation and deflation. The muscles of the lower circumference should by now be flexible, responsive, and sensitive. Flexing them even slightly should evoke an effective response. However, occasional conscientious repetition of the earlier exercises will prevent these muscles from becoming sloppy and unresponsive.

LESSON SIX

Applying the Breath

In the twenty-six exercises of the first five lessons, we have covered just about all the important muscular maneuvers that can help induce abdominal deep breathing and lead to an awareness of core energy.

Lesson 6 includes many earlier exercises, reviewing them to reveal further benefits that might not have been obvious during previous executions.

The following imagery drill is designed to deepen your inhalations and extend your exhalations.

IMAGERY DRILL

Book Stacking

Form the mental image of inhaling as a process of stacking books. You start stacking at the bottom, adding books to build a pile. The taller the stack, the more weight the bottom book has to bear. For exhalation, you unload the books from the top, working your way to the bottom book, which remains until the very end. You can stack or unstack rapidly or slowly, so long as you do the job steadily.

From now on, the position of the tip of your tongue as you breathe is less critical, as long as the tip of the tongue touches the front teeth. This position ensures that the tongue is not pulled back to obstruct the flow of air at the back of the throat. A relaxed tongue is always important in deep breathing.

The imagery drill that follows tests your ability to apply the energy that your core can now generate.

Facial Glow

1. Hold a mirror in front of you, and look into it.

2. Take an easy, deep breath, and exhale.

3. Look deeply into your own eyes as you take a long, deep breath and exhale.

4. Put the mirror down, but keep your eyes straight ahead.

5. Think about smiling. Take another easy deep breath, and exhale.

6. Sweep your glance upward, tilting your head back as you inhale deeply through your nose.

7. Hold your breath, and let it surround your core for a moment.

8. Exhale slowly and steadily through your nose as you imagine a warm glow emanating from your core. At the same time, sweep your glance back down, and level your head.

9. Break into a big smile, think a happy thought, and complete your exhalation.

10. Inhale and exhale as you smile. Feel your eyes sparkle, grow warm, and shine.

11. You are looking radiant!

12. Relaxed and content, proceed to Exercise 27.

Strengthening the Abdominal Muscles

Raising your arms high and pointing your fingers upward helps you stretch the entire length of your torso as much as possible.

Spreading your feet far apart helps broaden and stabilize the torso base, but in doing so you risk swaying your back and curving out the lower spine. To minimize this risk, stretch your entire top body up as straight as possible. At the same time, pull your abdomen slightly inward even before exhalation begins.

1. Stand up straight with your feet apart as far as possible without losing your balance. Point your toes slightly outward.

2. Raise your arms high, stretching your fingers toward the ceiling, palms forward (see Figure 75).

FIGURE 75

3. Exhale completely, doing the following steps simultaneously:

   ☐ Bend over and touch your toes (see Figure 76). If you can't touch your toes, bend as far as you can.

   ☐ Deflate the lower abdomen.

4. Inhale slowly, filling from the bottom up, doing the following steps simultaneously:

   ☐ Stand up slowly, stretching your arms and hands above your head (see Figure 77).

   ☐ Inflate the lower circumference.

5. Repeat steps 3 and 4 five times.

6. Remain standing with your hands reaching high. Exhale.

7. Hold still for 3 seconds; then lower your hands.

8. Inhale deeply, exhale, and relax.

FIGURE 77

FIGURE 76

EXERCISE 28

Strengthening the Lower Back Muscles

This exercise meets the same objectives as Exercise 27. Notice, however, that the emphasis shifts from the abdomen to the lower back torso by reversing the inhalation-exhalation procedure.

1. Stand up straight with your feet apart as far as possible without losing your balance. Point your toes slightly outward.

2. Raise your arms high above your head, stretching your fingers toward the ceiling, palms forward (see Figure 78). Exhale completely through your mouth.

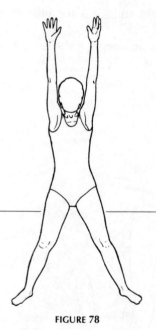

FIGURE 78

3. Inhale slowly from the bottom up, doing the following simultaneously:

   ☐ Bend over and touch your toes (see Figure 79). If you can't touch your toes, bend as far as you can.

   ☐ Inflate the lower circumference.

4. Exhale completely through your mouth, doing the following simultaneously:

   ☐ Stand up slowly, stretching your arms and hands toward the ceiling.

   ☐ Deflate the lower abdomen.

5. Repeat steps 3 and 4 five times.

6. Remain standing with your arms stretched high. Inhale deeply.

7. Hold your breath for a second.

8. Lower your hands, exhale, and relax.

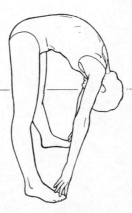

FIGURE 79

REVIEW EXERCISE 12 FROM LESSON 3, EXERCISE 10 FROM LESSON 2,
AND EXERCISE 17 FROM LESSON 3

Exercises 12, 10, and 17 demonstrate a progression of postures. Apply the following imagery drill during your review.

IMAGERY DRILL

Cream

Create a mental picture of an inhaled breath that is a rich, heavy liquid. On exhaling, leave behind the richness, and let the creaminess stick to the core, where it is converted into energy. You are learning to regulate and absorb that precious energy.

EXERCISE 29

Strengthening the Core

The breathing action that accompanies this movement thoroughly exercises the diaphragm and stimulates the core.

Steps 3 and 4 may seem difficult. Simply alternate moving your fists up and down as you swing your hips. Bending your knees and tipping your toes helps maintain balance and accommodate easy swaying. In this movement the midtorso, where the diaphragm is located, is being squeezed and stretched on alternate sides to develop flexibility.

1. Stand up straight with your feet spread apart to the width of your shoulders. Raise your arms out to the sides at shoulder height; then bend your elbows upward at right angles. Keep your elbows level with your shoulders. Tighten your hands into fists, palms facing forward (see Figure 80). Exhale completely, deflating the lower abdomen.

2. Inhale slowly, deeply, and fully. Hold your breath. Tighten the rectal muscle, pulling slightly upward. Then swallow, maintaining core tension.

FIGURE 80

3. Keep your rectal muscle tight while blowing forcefully in two consecutive big puffs, deflating the lower abdomen. At the first puff, simultaneously:

□ Pull your right fist downward, and push your left fist upward.

□ Swing your right hip to the right.

□ Bend your left knee slightly forward, raising your left foot on tiptoe (see Figure 81).

At the second puff, simultaneously:

□ Push your right fist upward, and pull your left fist downward.

□ Swing your left hip to the left.

□ Bend your right knee slightly forward, raising your right foot on tiptoe (see Figure 82).

4. Inhale through your nose forcefully in two consecutive sniffs, inflating the lower abdomen. At the first sniff, simultaneously:

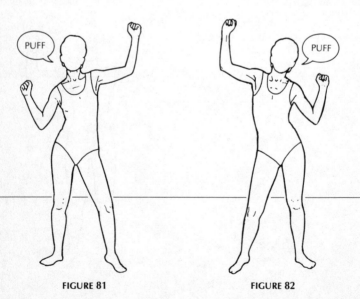

FIGURE 81　　　　　　　　**FIGURE 82**

☐ Pull your right fist downward, and push your left fist upward.

☐ Swing your right hip to the right.

☐ Bend your left knee slightly forward, raising your left foot on tiptoe (see Figure 83).

At the second sniff, simultaneously:

☐ Push your right fist upward, and pull your left fist downward.

☐ Swing your left hip to the left.

☐ Bend your right knee slightly forward, raising your right foot on tiptoe (see Figure 84).

5. Repeat steps 3 and 4 ten times, maintaining a tightened rectal muscle. End with an inhalation; level your shoulders and elbows.

6. Exhale slowly, lowering your hands to your sides.

7. Inhale, exhale, and relax.

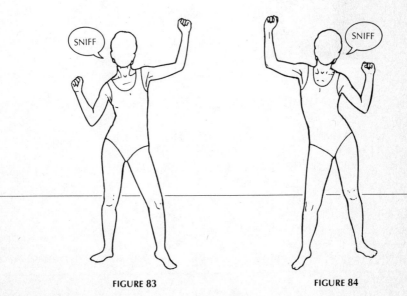

FIGURE 83   FIGURE 84

Exercise 29 was a rigorous exercise that placed great emphasis on the midtorso. Forgetting the lower torso and core can make it difficult for the breath to reach its necessary depth. A review of Exercises 26 and 25 will readjust any displacement that may have occurred. Reverse the original order of the exercises for your review; Exercise 25 will leave your body ready for Exercise 30.

EXERCISE 30

Jogging in Place with Chi Yi

All movement is affected by our manner of breathing. Jogging in place offers *one example* of the application of *chi yi*, showing how, in combination with various stages of physical exercise, you can experiment for improved results through the proper coordination of breathing and exercise.

1. Stand up straight with one foot flat on the floor and the other raised on tiptoe in a stationary jogging position. Keep your arms and hands in a position comfortable for running. Your hands should be loose and relaxed (see Figure 85).

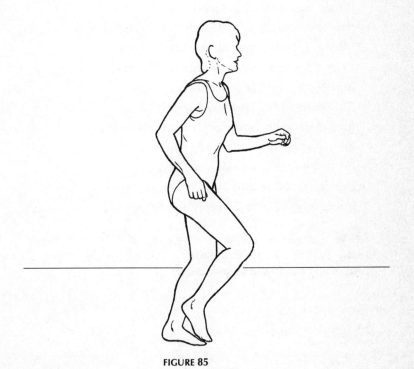

FIGURE 85

2. Throughout this exercise you will breathe in a natural way through the point where the back of the nose and the throat meet. Hold your teeth slightly apart, with your jaws relaxed. Place the tip of your tongue lightly behind your bottom front teeth.

3. Begin stationary jogging, slowly and steadily. Deflate the lower abdomen when exhaling, and inflate the lower circumference when inhaling. Alternately exhale and inhale in the following pattern:

   ☐ Exhale smoothly and steadily for 4 steps.
   ☐ Inhale smoothly and deeply for 4 steps.
   ☐ Exhale smoothly and steadily for 6 steps.
   ☐ Inhale smoothly and deeply for 6 steps.
   ☐ Exhale smoothly and steadily for 8 steps.
   ☐ Inhale smoothly and deeply for 8 steps.
   ☐ Exhale smoothly and steadily for 10 steps.
   ☐ Inhale smoothly and deeply for 10 steps.
   ☐ Exhale smoothly and steadily for 8 steps.
   ☐ Inhale smoothly and deeply for 8 steps.
   ☐ Exhale smoothly and steadily for 6 steps.
   ☐ Inhale smoothly and deeply for 6 steps.
   ☐ Exhale smoothly and steadily for 4 steps.
   ☐ Inhale smoothly and deeply for 4 steps.
   ☐ Exhale smoothly and steadily for 10 steps.
   ☐ Inhale smoothly and deeply for 10 steps.

4. As you continue stationary jogging, slowly and easily adapt to your normal breathing pattern while bringing your steps gradually to a standstill.

Thoughts on Lesson 6

The most important objective of this lesson is to develop a keener awareness of the core and to apply this awareness to *any* activity. By the time you have completed this lesson, the muscles involved in *chi yi* should respond readily to your commands. Feel free to improvise new routines, and to incorporate what you have learned into your daily activities.

Frequently review those exercises that are most effective for you. Do not overlook or underestimate the exercises in the beginning lessons; each one has its particular value.

Be patient and persistent in your practice and application of *chi yi*. Your painstaking effort at the beginning will gradually become spontaneous, and eventually you will find shallow breathing to be uncomfortable, ineffective, and unnatural. It is then that you will recognize that you have mastered the art of breathing.

You may have noticed that your natural breathing patterns sometimes have suspended (rest) intervals between exhalations and inhalations. The length of these suspended intervals depends mainly on the physical and sometimes on the mental and emotional demands at the time. A natural instinct usually takes care of such adjustments. For instance, in running the intervals will be very short. In walking, you may experience an interval to a count of 1 or 2, depending on the amount of energy exerted and the amount of air inhaled and exhaled. In resting, you may experience 3 counts inhale, 3 counts exhale, 3 counts suspended interval. When you are asleep, the suspended period will be extended. Understanding this fact will facilitate the adaptation of *chi yi* into whatever you do.

PART THREE

Applications of Chi Yi

Using the Core Energy

Once you have completed the six lessons outlined in Part 2 of this book, you will have established a strong, sound foundation in *chi yi*. As with all worthwhile skills, the techniques involved must be consistently practiced to maintain the art of breathing. Successful results depend on continued effort and mastery of all the lessons.

Now that your core awareness is well established, you are equipped to function more effectively in every area of your life. The applications that follow will show you how *chi yi* techniques may be applied to the endeavors of daily life, and how they enhance the health and well-being of those who practice them. Once you have worked with these applications, you will be able to adapt them to create your own program of *chi yi* practice.

Disciplined inner energy helps you to realize your full human potential. Uncontrolled inner energy creates tension and stress. It is impossible simply to discard unwanted tension and stress. You must *relocate* them. The practice of *chi yi* enables you to direct unwanted tension and stress to the core, from which it can be circulated throughout the body as beneficial energy.

Now that you have mastered the basic techniques of *chi yi* set forth in the progressive exercises of Part 2, the Steam Funnel Imagery Drill will further assist you in the circulation of inner energy. Keep this image in mind as you practice the applications in Part 3.

In this imagery drill, imagining your inhaled breath as water facilitates the feeling of the breath's flowing downward and hitting bottom. Imagining your exhaled breath as warm water and steam being pumped upward allows you to sense how the breath lingers during the exhalation. As you practice this exercise, you are likely to sense the warm inner energy flowing to your face and head area. Imagining the inner energy as a warm current provides a vivid sensation that can be easily traced and monitored.

IMAGERY DRILL

Steam Funnel

Think of the back of your nose, at the point where it meets the throat, as the top of a funnel emptying into a long tube that leads all the way down to a focal area where a rotating propeller sits ready to spin (see Figure 86). As you begin an inhalation, imagine the air you breathe as water pouring into the funnel and draining down to start the rotor spinning. Let the rotor gain momentum for a few seconds, heating up and setting off an energy that radiates and sparkles and, at the same time, gives off enough power to propel an exhalation in the form of warm water and steam.

It is this return column of energized air that triggers and manipulates the voice. This energized exhalation also gives your face an attractive glow.

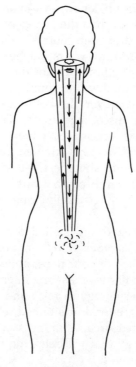

FIGURE 86

During exhalations, you gain the benefit of your inhalations, allowing you to target your inner energy to the body areas that need it most. You can most effectively direct your inner energy with your mind and imagination during the exhalation. You need not have a plan for every exhalation; most of the time it is natural to let your inner energy circulate freely so that your entire being can benefit from it.

Flourishing inner energy naturally attends to the most pressing needs of the various parts of your body. For instance, if you are extremely tired and lie down to rest, you may feel your inner energy throbbing at the parts of your body that are most strained, such as the base of your neck, your head, your legs, and so on. Encourage such sensations with *chi yi* breathing; they will help you to recuperate.

The surges of inner energy may be perceived as throbs, as patches of inner warmth, or as rays or flashes of inner light. These throbs are slower than the pulses of the heart, occurring about one per second or even more slowly. If these sensations come to you in the form of warm patches or light flashes and so have a less vivid rhythm, monitor them by mentally counting at the speed of roughly one count per second.

Whenever and wherever throbbing sensations occur—not painful ones—don't discourage them. They are a sign that your inner energy is surging to where it's needed in your body. For instance, if you have strained muscles at the base of your neck and in your shoulders, lie down and do *chi yi* breathing. Soon you will become aware of a throbbing sensation in that strained area, gradually bringing on relief and comfort.

After you have talked and smiled continuously for a long time, relax and focus your mind on your tired lips, jaws, gums, and on the back of your nose, and you will sense these muscles, bones, and tissues pulsating intensely. They are being helped by your inner energy to relax and recuperate.

When your eyes are tired or strained, close them and bring your attention to that area. Your eyes will be soothed with pulsating inner energy that will relax the eyes themselves and the surrounding muscles.

Painful throbbing is a signal from the body of some injury, tension, or stress. You will learn to blend these throbs with your inner energy surges to dispel pain and tension.

To encourage your awareness of the throbbing sensation created by the concentration of inner energy, practice the following imagery drill.

IMAGERY DRILL

Sink and Drain

Inhale as if you are filling up a sink from the bottom upward. Exhale as if you are draining a sink through the bottom. Repeat these two steps a few times. Then suspend your breathing for a few seconds, and concentrate on developing a slow throb in your core. Resume breathing as you continue to monitor your throbs. Apply this throbbing sensation to various areas of the body by mentally moving the throbs from the core to other parts of your body.

Suggestions for Practicing the Applications

When you are practicing the applications, remember always to invigorate and back up your inner energy with deep inhalations and lingering exhalations. *Chi yi* breaths may vary in intensity and frequency. As you monitor your throbs, light flashes, or warm patches, your breaths may at times become so faint and infrequent that they seem hardly to be there.

These faint inhalations will be interspersed with some long, intense inhalations whenever your body feels the need. Let your natural instincts be your guide. If the throbs or sensations of light or warmth should hesitate or fade away, regenerate them with a few intense, regulated exhalations and inhalations, almost like deep sighs. Use the Sink and Drain Imagery Drill to encourage these sensations. Whether your breaths are faint or intense, frequent or sparse, the most important point to remember is to inhale to the core and to let your exhalations linger.

You can bring on the sensations of inner energy surges with *chi yi* breathing and exaggerated flexing of the lower abdominal muscles, which stimulates the core. Deep breathing can also be induced with vivid mental pictures, as in the imagery drill below.

Drinking Straw

Imagine an oversized drinking straw with one end at the nose-throat junction and the other end leading to the center of the core. Both ends are kept open at all times to allow the air to flow freely. As you inhale, imagine air being sucked in through the lower opening, inflating the lower abdomen. Stop, and reverse your mental gears in preparation for exhalation. Now imagine the straw with air flowing out through both ends (without collapsing the straw at any point). Exhale completely. Then proceed again with another inhalation.

The following core awareness imagery drill also cultivates and helps you channel the core's energy. It will be put to use in several of the applications that follow.

Red Light Bulb

Do your *chi yi* breathing as you imagine, as vividly as you can, an electric socket at the location of your core. Screw a red light bulb into this socket, and watch it light up. Imagine that the light glows evenly as you exhale and inhale deeply and smoothly. At the pauses between exhalations and inhalations, or when you hold your breath, the light does not flicker or go out, but sustains an even glow.

As soon as *chi yi* is thoroughly integrated into your life, as you work or play or engage in physical activities throughout the day, you may apply an exercise or drill to help you relax or to act more effectively. Throughout the day and night, you will find yourself breathing more deeply, with greater ease. You are enjoying *chi yi*—the art of breathing.

APPLICATION 1

Promoting Relaxation

Whenever you are under pressure, or in a rush, or feeling tense, let *chi yi* help you take stock of the situation. Loosen and lower your shoulders. Breathe to your core, and let your breath linger and filter downward. Do this several times, until you feel your taut nerves and muscles loosen up. You will find that you are better able to control your feelings, and to be more patient, tolerant, and pleasant than before.

Anxiety can be greatly eased or even eliminated by bringing your inner energy throbs to the spot at the center of your chest just below the point where your front ribs meet. Concentrate your inner energy surges there, and let them warm that spot and loosen the knots there. Soon your anxiety will begin to evaporate.

1. Take a few deep breaths to firmly establish an inner vision of the core's location.

2. Analyze and trace your points of tension.

3. Continue breathing deeply and steadily as you direct imaginary lumps of tension, one at a time, to the core and calmly drop them into the core's cradle to dissolve.

4. Tension often gathers at the back of the neck and shoulders, contributing to aches and pains in the arms and from the head down through the spine. To relieve that neck-shoulder tension, check the following vital points, and follow the prescribed remedies.

   □ Tongue. If your tongue is persistently pulled back, away from the front teeth, tension will be created in the jaw and neck. Remedy this condition by pushing the tongue forward gently, filling up the space behind the lower front teeth. Then let the tongue go limp, and breathe.

   □ Shoulders. When your shoulders are heaved (raised), you are fighting against gravity. Seesaw and rotate your shoulders a few times; then smooth your shoulders backward and downward, and breathe comfortably.

APPLICATION 2

Waking Up Alert:
The Good Morning Regimen

For many people, just waking up and getting out of bed in the morning requires quite an effort and, in fact, may be very stressful. Many rely on a cup of black coffee or an extra half-hour in bed to become their usual social selves. They hope to become alert, bright-eyed, and radiant as the day goes by.

This *chi yi* regimen prepares you for getting out of bed with all your faculties fully functioning. The regimen requires you to stay in bed for 10 minutes or so after you awaken. If you wake up by the alarm clock, set it 10 minutes earlier. You will get out of bed much less blurry-eyed and cranky than you would have after those extra 10 minutes of sleep. This *chi yi* application requires willpower on your part, but you will find the reward more than worth the effort.

At first glance, the regimen may look long and complicated. After you review it a few times, you will find it systematic and easy to remember. Memorize the steps or at least understand and organize them in your mind before you actually do the regimen.

The number of throbs indicated in this application is to be considered a guideline. Use your discretion in this matter according to your physical condition and the time you have allotted for performing the regimen. You can mentally direct inner energy sensations and channel them to whatever location you desire. For instance, if you have a stuffy nose, a sore throat, or an uncomfortable stomach, you will want to let the throbs linger in the sensitive area.

When you wake up in the morning, remain lying in bed with your eyes closed. If you need to make a trip to the bathroom, return immediately to bed. If your room is cool, keep the covers over you so that you are comfortable and warm. You may bend your knees if that position is more comfortable than lying flat. At first you may find lying on your back easier than any other position, but as you become more experienced, you may find it just as easy to perform the regimen lying on either side, as long as you are relaxed and comfortable.

Remember always to invigorate and back up your inner energy with deep inhalations and lingering exhalations.

1. Lie comfortably in bed with your eyes closed.

2. Do the Eyedropper Imagery Drill from Part 1 to refresh the deep breathing sensation.

3. Relax your hands and elbows. Rest your hands one over the other on your lower abdomen. Let your elbows rest on the bed beside your body.

4. Flex your lower abdominal muscles and vigorously deflate the abdomen as you exhale by blowing rapidly through slightly pursed lips. Relax your abdominal muscle; it will pop outward, effecting a rapid, deep inhalation of air. Do this in/out process of flexing the abdominal wall to the count of 1-2. Repeat the process 10 times in succession, ending with a long, slow, deep inhalation followed by a long, slow, thorough exhalation.

5. Relax. Monitor your body for throbs or pulsations. You may sense them at many areas of your body, especially around your eye sockets, between your cheeks and gums, at the back of your nose, and in your neck, your inner shoulders, and your lower abdomen. If you are aware of no such sensations, repeat step 4. If you still have no reaction, do the Simplified Vowel Exercise that appears on page 155. Then proceed to step 6.

6. Concentrate on throbs in one area at a time, starting with the lower abdomen. Mentally direct the throbs to your tailbone. Inch them slowly up the spine to the top of your head (the crown).

7. Mentally direct the throbs toward the eye sockets. Monitor 20 throbs there.

8. Direct 10 to 14 throbs to the center of the bridge of the nose. If you have a stuffy nose, let the throbs dwell longer at that area, and the stuffiness may disappear.

9. Direct 10 to 14 throbs to the tip of your nose.

10. Direct 10 to 14 throbs to your upper gum.

11. Let 10 to 14 throbs spread to your cheeks. You may feel a flush spreading through the center of your face. Direct 10 throbs to that area.

12. Direct 10 to 14 throbs each to your lower gum, tongue, and chin.

13. Direct 10 to 14 throbs to your throat. If you have a sore throat, allow the throbs to dwell at the throat area to soothe away the pain. If a ticklish feeling in the throat is bringing on a cough, hold off the cough as long as you can. Allow the throbs to dwell at that location until the tickling sensation subsides.

14. Direct 10 to 14 throbs to the base of the neck and across the inner shoulders. If you are suffering from a stiff neck or strained shoulders, let the throbs dwell in the neck-shoulder area to relieve tension.

15. Direct throbs in little steps, one throb per step, down the center front of your body. Let the throbs dwell at whatever spot feels tight, uncomfortable, or uneasy. Throbbing in the abdominal area may at times start your stomach rumbling; it may even cause you to pass gas. This response is a good sign; it shows that your stomach is waking up, too! Aim your throbs toward the lower abdomen.

16. Rub your warm hands over your abdomen and the front of your rib cage, gently massaging these areas. Enjoy this stimulation for a few seconds, or longer if you wish.

17. Sit up. Put your feet on the floor.

18. Dangle your head and roll it to the right in big circles slowly 4 times, synchronizing the motion with the breath—inhale-exhale-inhale-exhale. Repeat the process, rolling your head to the left.

19. Bring your right palm to the left side of the base of your neck. Pat gently and firmly, starting at the base of the neck, moving along the left shoulder and down the arm

toward the hand and fingers. Pat more at the spots where you feel tension. Repeat this patting motion 2 times.

Note: During the process of directing the inner energy surges up and down your head and torso in steps 1 through 16, your limbs may have become tense. The patting will relieve any tension. And more importantly, the stimulation of the patting will lead the flow of inner energy you have activated during steps 1 through 16 to the limbs as well.

20. Bring your left palm to the right side of the base of your neck. Pat gently and firmly, starting at the base of the neck, moving along the right shoulder and down the arm toward the hand and fingers. Again, pat more at any tense spots. Repeat this patting motion 2 times.

21. Again bring your right palm to the left side of the base of your neck. Pat along the shoulder to the top of the left arm. At this point, turn your left palm outward, bringing the inside of your left arm outward also. Continue patting downward along the inside of the left arm to the palm, ending at the fingertips. Repeat this patting motion 2 times.

22. Again bring your left palm to the right side of the base of your neck. Pat along the shoulder to the top of the right arm. At this point, turn your right palm outward, bringing the inside of your right arm outward also. Continue patting downward along the inside of the right arm to the palm, ending at the fingertips. Repeat this patting motion 2 times.

23. Stand up. Dangle your hands in front of you and shake them vigorously 20 times.

24. Stand up straight with your feet spread comfortably, 16 to 18 inches apart. Bring your right hand to your left underarm with the palm inward, fingers pointing backward. Gently and firmly pat downward on the left side of your body to the left hip; then proceed toward the center of your lower abdomen. Repeat this patting motion 2 times.

25. In the same standing position, bring your left hand to your right underarm with the palm inward, fingers pointing backward. Gently and firmly pat downward on the right side of your body toward the right hip, and proceed to pat toward the lower center of the abdomen. Repeat this patting motion 2 times.

26. Stand upright with your feet slightly parted, 8 to 10 inches apart. Bring your hands to the sides of your hips, palms inward, fingers pointing toward the center of your back. Gently and firmly pat slowly toward the center lower back, and proceed downward along the backs of your legs to your heels. Bend down gradually as you pat, then straighten up. Repeat this patting motion 2 times.

27. Bend forward with your feet parted at slightly wider than shoulder's width. Bring your hands to your crotch (the very top of the inside of your legs) with the palm inward, fingers pointing backward. Gently and firmly pat downward along the inside of your legs toward the inside ankles, bending down gradually as you pat. Stand up. Repeat this patting motion 2 times.

28. Walk in place or around the room 30 to 40 steps, lifting your feet high. Now you are all set for a good day, with bright eyes and rosy cheeks, full of energy.

Whenever you have the luxury of relaxing in bed for a few extra minutes, take the opportunity to improve your weak areas. For example, if you are susceptible to lower back pain, lie on your side with your knees drawn up in the fetal position. Focus your mind on your lower back. Take a few *chi yi* breaths, then direct your throbs (or patches of warmth, or flashes of light) to your lower back. Let these sensations dwell at the painful area for as long as you like. You may focus your mind on and send your inner energy to soothe and repair any spot in your body—a joint in your finger, a strained calf muscle, or your teeth and gums.

To start the day with a rosy glow, bring the throbs to your face in order to stimulate your skin and facial muscles.

APPLICATION 3

Motivating Movement from the Core

This application of *chi yi* shows you how to make connections between your movements and your core. Breathing affects your core, which in turn affects your movements. If you are lucky, your movements may be instinctively motivated from the core, whether or not you realize how that came about. However, the more fully you understand and exercise your ability to move from the core, the more you can control your movements and improve them at will.

After you have practiced this application, you will find that you are more aware of every movement you make, and you will move with more control. Your penmanship may even improve! At first, practice this application for short periods (5 to 10 minutes). This technique of control will gradually blend into your everyday movements, naturally and easily. Your movements will become more graceful, more steady, and more confident.

1. Stand with your feet 10 to 12 inches apart, toes pointed slightly outward. Hold your hands behind your back, and let them dangle loosely.

2. Inhale deeply, and exhale thoroughly. Inhale again easily, and continue breathing without further attention to your breathing process.

3. Tighten your lower abdominal muscle, and lift the center of the torso floor.

4. Do the Red Light Bulb Imagery Drill. Imagine as vividly as you can an electric socket at the location of your core. Screw a little red light bulb into this socket and watch it light up. Imagine the glowing bulb.

5. Raise on tiptoe and lower yourself several times. As you do this, imagine that the bulb glows with each lift. The more strength your movement requires, the brighter the bulb glows.

6. Place your feet more widely apart. Shift your weight from one foot to the other a few times. As you do this, imagine that the bulb glows more intensely as the movement demands greater energy.

7. Walk around the room. Imagine that the bulb brightens and dims as you pick up and lower your feet and shift your weight.

8. Raise one arm to your head. Notice the reactions of the bulb. Draw big round circles in the air with your hand. Lower your hand gracefully to your side. This movement also takes energy to control. Imagine how the bulb brightens and dims as any part of you moves. Raise your other arm, and put it through various motions. Pick up objects from the table, and put them back down. Mentally watch the reactions of the bulb.

9. Turn your head to one side. Lift it. Turn it to the other side. Keep an image of the bulb in your mind as you move.

10. Make any movement with any part of your body. Lift and wiggle a finger. Roll your eyes. Write with a pencil. Maintain the imagery of the bulb glowing in its various intensities.

APPLICATION 4

Developing Athletic Prowess

The previous application, which develops motivated movements, will adapt easily and beneficially to all your athletic
activities. Athletic movements require much more exact execution, strength, and coordination than do the movements of
everyday actions. At first you may feel that the application
interferes with your spontaneity and natural reflexes; and it
may, until you make the technique part of your subconscious
mind. If practiced faithfully, however, this technique will soon
become spontaneous, and will greatly enhance your athletic
movements.

All sports require footwork of some sort. Your steps determine the direction, position, and maneuverability of your entire body. Experiments scrutinizing runners' patterns of
running and breathing at various stages of a run, under various conditions, and at different speeds, have concluded that
synchronization takes place between pace and breath. The
speed of a runner depends on both the rate and the length of
his or her stride. Experiments have shown that even when
runners aim for a longer stride, their phase-locked pattern of
breathing and footsteps need not change. Scientists are continuing to study phase-locked breathing and running patterns.

A 1983 article by Dennis M. Bramble and David R. Carrier
(*Science*, Vol. 219, 21 January 1983, p. 251) recorded that four-
legged animals normally synchronize their footfalls and their
breathing cycles for trots and gallops at a constant 1:1 ratio
(one stride per breath). Human runners employ several phase-
locked patterns (4:1, 3:1, 2:1, 1:1, 5:2, 3:2), although the 2:1
pattern seems to be the most commonly used. In whatever
pattern, the synchronization of breathing and physical movements appears to be necessary during sustained running.

If a phase-locked pattern of movement and breathing is necessary for sustained running, it must also be important for not-
so-sustained running, and it may well be helpful in walking in
regulated steps. In fact, a phase-locked pattern between
breathing and any movement of the body can effect better performance. These patterns, however, vary under different conditions and with different people. No formula has been

established for getting the best results. You, or you and your coach, will work out what is best for you.

Where does the runner get the extra energy required for longer strides? I believe that the principles of *chi yi* offer an answer to how the runner gets extra energy: Deeper breathing stimulates the core to produce more inner energy.

Sports vary greatly in their degree of rhythmic involvement. In general, noncompetitive sports—jogging, bicycling, aerobic exercises, rope skipping, skating, and so on—are more highly regulated by rhythm. Competitive sports that engage opponents and require teamwork—tennis, football, baseball, and so on—are usually freer from set rhythms. The more rhythmic the sport, the more your performance can benefit from phase-locked patterns of breathing and movement.

This application will show you how to generate and direct inner energy when participating in athletic activities.

1. Strike the stance that you would normally take as you begin practicing your sport.

2. If an instrument such as a racket is involved, hold it as you normally would at the starting point.

3. Take a *chi yi* breath (exhalation and inhalation).

4. Inhale, and hold your breath without straining. Touch your top and bottom teeth together, but don't bite hard. Place the tip of your tongue against your front teeth.

5. Produce a sustained *tse* sound. To make sure that this sound does not bring on tension of the neck or shoulder muscles, roll your head clockwise and counter-clockwise several times as you proceed with your continuous *tse* sound.

6. As you continue making the *tse* sound, you will feel your core tightening and generating energy. Sustaining the sound, think of the Red Light Bulb Imagery Drill with the bulb plugged into the socket. Imagine the light of the red bulb glowing steadily—as steady as your *tse*—until the end of this exhalation.

7. Inhale.

8. Exhale in the form of disconnected short *tse* syllables. As you exhale, do the following simultaneously:

◻ Do the movements of your sport—swing your racket, take a step, jump, swing, or the like—in a slightly slow motion.

◻ Accompany each movement with a *tse* sound and a profuse glow of the imaginary red bulb. (You can do this step when you are actually playing the game just for practice.)

9. Continue to inhale and exhale freely, at the rate and intensity at which you feel comfortable. As you exhale, the disconnected *tse* sounds should accompany your actions; let the core bulb glow to accompany your *tse* sounds.

10. Continue with steps 7, 8, and 9 as long as you wish and as long as you feel comfortable doing them.

APPLICATION 5

Sustaining Personal Presence

Most virtuoso performers are able to attract the attention of their audience, but the greatest virtuosos are those who can maintain a continuous magnetism so that members of the audience can't take their eyes or ears from them even when they pause. This ability to deliver a skill laced with continuous magnetism adds a charismatic quality to every note, phrase, line, and movement they send forth—a string of perfected pearls strung together not with string but with magnetic inner energy.

Applications 3 and 4 teach you to direct your inner energy to your physical expression and movements. This application shows you how to develop an inner energy capable of sustaining and molding itself so that it corresponds with the demands of artistic performance and stage presence. You may apply this energy to your performance in any situation, in the conference room or on the stage.

First, do the Red Light Bulb Imagery Drill. We will work with the image of the red electric bulb plugged in at your lower abdomen, at the location of your core. Not only must you be able mentally to turn it on and off, but when you are performing, you must know how to keep it on all the time. You don't want it at full power continuously; you want to be able to manipulate its glow as though it had a dimmer switch.

Basically, you must learn to overcome the break between exhalation and inhalation. Your imaginary bulb has a natural tendency to go off at that moment of transition, so that you must mentally make the light come back on after the interruption. This takes additional effort, and you may momentarily lose your audience.

This application helps you overcome the interference of this sporadic "darkness" in the breathing cycle. The steps sound simple, but the application is difficult; it can be mentally exhausting. Be careful not to overpractice, especially at first; 10 or 20 seconds may be enough for beginners. Eventually, however, the application will become a spontaneous part of your skill in appearing before people. Your diligence will be greatly rewarded.

1. Do the Red Light Bulb Imagery Drill.

2. Exhale, as you imagine the light burning brightly.

3. As you approach the end of your exhalation, mentally turn the light bulb to tighten its contact with the socket, and make sure that the light does not flicker, dim, or go off.

4. Inhale without the slightest flickering of the light. Continue inhaling, and keep the light shining.

5. As you approach the end of your inhalation, again mentally turn the light bulb slightly to reassert its contact with the socket. Make sure that the light does not flicker or dim.

6. Repeat steps 2 through 5 as many times as you can manage without overexerting mentally.

APPLICATION 6

Working through Pain

The painful throbs you experience when you are in pain are SOS signals for immediate attention. Do not ignore those throbbing pains. They are calling for the mind to direct inner energy to that area. When your mind focuses on an area of your body, inner energy can be directed to that place to perform its function of soothing, healing, and strengthening. The length of time it takes the pain to ebb away depends on the degree of affliction.

1. Take several deep, full inhalations and lingering, thorough exhalations.

2. Focus your mind on any throbbing pains. Monitor them by mentally counting as you continue with your *chi yi* breathing. Count in a simple sequence such as 1 through 4, or 1 through 10. Repeat the sequence to avoid high numbers with many syllables, which tend to interfere with a free-flowing rhythm.

3. Continue to count. Before long, you will find the pain subsiding and the throbs becoming regular and painless throbs of inner energy.

APPLICATION 7

Relieving Discomfort in the Fingers, Hands, and Arms

You can use *chi yi* to relieve muscle aches in the limbs. For example, if your elbow aches, bring on the inner energy throbbing sensation. Stimulate a few throbs of pain at the elbow by bending or pressing it. Synchronize the energy throbs with the painful throbs in your elbow, while letting your entire arm relax and go limp. Maintain your *chi yi* breathing. The throbs of pain will very quickly become plain throbs. Monitor the throbs at the elbow for at least 50 to 100 counts. At the end of this count you will find your pain much relieved, if not completely gone. Your first few tries may not bring on very conspicuous positive results. Give this approach several chances, taking a little rest time between attempts. Repeat this therapy whenever necessary.

This application can be done while you are lying down, sitting, or standing and in any surroundings—in front of a TV set or in a concert hall—as long as your hands are free.

During this application, your inner energy will stimulate the painful areas and cut through any interference that may stagnate the flow of the inner energy current. Let us say, for example, that the joints in your left index finger are painful, due to strain or arthritis.

1. Warm your right hand in any convenient way. Put it in your pocket, or hold it under your coat or your sweater, or even in your armpit.

2. Wrap your warm right hand over your left index finger, gripping it firmly but without squeezing.

3. In seconds you will feel your left index finger throbbing together with your right hand. You are feeling the pulses of your heartbeat. These heart beats, at about 70 to 80 per minute, are faster than the throbs created by your inner energy, at about 45 to 55 per minute.

4. Monitor the heart-related throbs for about 30 seconds.

5. Loosen the grip of your right hand to an easy hold. Continue focusing your mind on your aching index finger.

6. The heart-related throbs will grow faint and, as they seem to be ebbing away, slower-paced throbs will emerge. Your inner energy surges are now taking over.

7. During steps 1 through 6 you have been breathing naturally in a *chi yi* manner and need not have given your breathing any thought. As you monitor the slower throbs, your breathing will adjust itself in rate, intensity, and quantity. At times your breathing may seem to have subsided to almost nothing; at other times you may feel the urge to take very deep, long inhalations. Let your instincts command your course. At this stage, you are equipped with adequate *chi yi* techniques to respond to any demand of breathing. If your inner energy throbs start to fade too soon, intentionally initiate several deep, long inhalations and lingering exhalations, which should strengthen the throbs again.

8. When you feel you can no longer concentrate or that the throbs have done their work, stop and relax.

9. During steps 6, 7, and 8, the pain in your finger should gradually have been eased and perhaps even eliminated. Although your finger may not hurt anymore, it may still feel stiff. Flex your left hand a few times, and massage it with your right.

10. Continue practicing this application frequently, with the intention of improving the condition of the ailing joints and preventing the recurrence of pain.

This approach to easing pain may also be practiced on your knees and upper thighs when you are in a sitting position and your hands can comfortably reach these areas.

APPLICATION 8
Conditioning the Legs and Arms

Our limbs are indispensable for a physically active life. For athletes, dancers, laborers, and many others, limbs are tools of the trade. Even when our limbs are healthy, it's still a good idea to give them some attention. We should develop the ability to lead our inner energy through our legs and arms, first to keep them healthy, and second to become familiar with the technique of directing inner energy through these areas. Then when our limbs need conditioning, soothing, or healing, we will be more adept and efficient at that task.

You can do this application while you watch TV or ride a bus, train, or plane; you can even do it during a dull lecture or conference, if no one is watching—you may look a little absent-minded. You can practice it while lying in bed, although if you are sitting up, it is easier for you to keep your eyes on the areas on which your mind's eye will also concentrate.

When you are thoroughly familiar with this application, you will not need the assistance of your eyesight to guide the movement of inner energy. You can direct and control the flow of inner energy with your mind's eye alone. As long as you are in a place where you are able to concentrate, you can practice this application inconspicuously anywhere and anytime.

It helps if you look at the spot you are concentrating on while you imagine with your mind's eye. Looking will help to induce the throbs or light flashes at that spot.

When your body and mind have become familiar with and adapted to this application, you may combine steps 2 through 6 with steps 7 and 8; that is, you may send inner energy up and down both legs simultaneously. You may also do the same with both arms.

1. Begin with a few *chi yi* breaths and bring on inner energy throbs in your lower abdomen.

2. Look at the top of your right leg.

3. Focus your mind's eye at the same spot at the top of your right leg.

4. Do a few more *chi yi* breaths as you concentrate on feeling a sensation at that spot on your leg. This sensation may be a throb, a warm patch, a flashing spot of light, or some other manifestation.

5. Using both your inner sight and outer sight, slowly guide this small patch of sensation down the length of your right leg to your ankle, foot, and toes. Mentally move this sensation along, down the leg, stopping every inch or so to tap that spot mentally in counts of 1-2 or 1-2-3-4. Dwell longer at the foot and toes by repeating more sequences of taps at each spot.

6. In the same way, return the sensation from your toes up to the top of your right leg (repeating step 5 in the reverse direction).

7. Now shift your inner and outer sight to the top of your left leg.

8. Focus, concentrate, and proceed as described in steps 2 through 6, applying these steps to the left leg.

9. Direct your inner energy sensation to your core. Let it pulse there for a bit. Relax, and rest for a moment.

Note: You may want to end the exercise at this point, or you may continue stimulating your arms by doing the following steps.

10. Direct your inner energy sensation from your core to the base of your neck. (If you had temporarily stopped and are now resuming this exercise, you will need to begin this step with a few *chi yi* breaths to get your inner energy going before you proceed.)

11. Place your right hand palm down in your lap. Look at the top of your right arm (at your right shoulder).

12. Focus your mind's eye at the same spot at the top of your right arm.

13. Concentrate on feeling a sensation at that spot. This sensation may be a throb, a warm patch, a flashing spot of light, or some other manifestation.

14. Using both your inner sight and outer sight, guide this small patch of sensation down the length of your right arm to your wrist, hand, and fingers. Mentally move the sensation along, down the arm, stopping every inch or so to tap that spot mentally in counts of 1-2 or 1-2-3-4. Dwell longer at the hand and fingers by repeating more sequences of taps at each spot.

15. In the same way, return the sensation to the top of your right shoulder (repeating step 14 in the reverse direction).

16. Now shift both your inner and outer sight to the top of your left arm (at your left shoulder). Place your left hand palm down in your lap.

17. Focus, concentrate, and proceed as described in steps 11 through 15, applying these steps to the left arm.

18. Roll your head in big circles, 5 times clockwise and 5 times counter-clockwise. Put both your hands over your lower abdomen.

19. Take several good stabilizing *chi yi* breaths, and relax.

Note: If you are interrupted during the course of this exercise, just take a few deep abdominal breaths to stabilize and anchor your inner energy. You may then proceed to any activity awaiting you.

APPLICATION 9

Creating a Dynamic Image

You had sufficient rest, and you are superbly dressed, yet you feel tired and drab, and you know that you look dull and project little vitality. You are on your way to a very important meeting, a photography session, an audition, an interview, or a party. You want to make an impact upon arrival. You are in your car on the way, or you are waiting for the elevator or in the reception room. You wish you could give yourself a lift. Try this application. You will feel a difference, and that difference will be visible to others.

1. Start your inner energy going by exhaling thoroughly and taking a long, deep inhalation. Imagine that you are deeply drawing in the scent of your favorite flower while also breathing through your mouth. Draw that inhalation into the very depth of you. Savor the fragrance of that inhalation for a few seconds before letting it drain out slowly.

2. Breathe in and out easily 3 times as you purposefully inflate and deflate your lower abdomen.

3. Take another long draw of fragrance, and repeat step 1.

4. Repeat steps 2 and 3 twice.

5. Your face will begin to feel warm, and your inner energy will start throbbing behind your nose and eyes. Let the throbs float through your face, your gums, the tip of your tongue, and your lips. You can almost feel a smile breaking out all over your countenance. Your face is glowing.

6. Take another long drag of air. Exhale by letting the air spill out all over.

7. You are sitting, standing, and walking tall, confident, and radiant. Keep your inner energy throbbing in your face and through your eyes as constantly as you can. You are looking great!

APPLICATION 10

Combatting Insomnia

Proper breathing can be applied as if it were a tonic for insomnia. First try Application 1, Promoting Relaxation. If that doesn't lull you to sleep, then capture your wandering thoughts by focusing on your abdominal breathing.

Individual sleep requirements vary; *chi yi* will not cause you to sleep naturally for much longer than your normal physical sleep requirement.

1. Breathe deeply to stimulate the core's cradle (the lower abdominal area), and to produce a throbbing sensation at the core. (Try the Tumbling Pebble Imagery Drill, page 15.)

2. Should you need additional stimulation to produce the pulsating sensation, vigorously pump your lower abdomen inward and outward 10 to 15 times, deflating as you exhale and inflating as you inhale.

3. When you have produced the throbbing sensation, focus your full attention on it.

4. As the throbbing gradually strengthens, it dominates your other sensations. Move the throbs to your thighs or toes. Imagine these throbbings as floating bubbles, *never* as bursting bubbles. Images of bursting bubbles will create an agitating effect. Notice that your breathing gradually becomes more subdued and slower, almost as though it were ebbing away. This ebbing, which produces a very calming effect, is to be encouraged.

5. When aches, pains, or discomfort are keeping you awake, extend this throbbing sensation from your core to the affected spot, allowing it to soothe and relieve the affliction.

6. Continue to monitor the throbs by counting them in repeated sequences of four, over and over. Before you realize it, you will fall asleep.

APPLICATION 11

Relieving Gas Pains in the Stomach

Gas pain is often caused by overeating or nervous tension. This application induces surges of core energy to relieve this discomfort.

Important: Be sure your symptoms are not caused by a heart condition, appendicitis, food poisoning, or any other ailment that requires the immediate attention of a physician.

1. Bring on inner energy throbbings with *chi yi* breathing.

2. Move your mind's eye to the uncomfortable spot in your stomach. Focus on that spot for a few seconds, until the throbbing begins there.

3. Monitor this throbbing for at least 50 to 100 counts.

4. You may also put your palms at the spot if your hands are warm; the warmth will encourage and intensify the throbs. You will feel rumbling at the affected area and will begin to burp and pass gas, and you will feel much better.

Relieving Congested Nasal Passages or Sinuses

At the first hint of discomfort, do the following:

1. After you sneeze or blow your nose, concentrate on feeling a throbbing at the facial mask area and the nose.

Note: With no sneeze or nose-blowing to start the throbbing sensation, begin by focusing your mind's eye on the affected spot. Then blow your nose.

2. Pick up on the rhythm of the throbbing, and monitor it.

3. At the same time, encourage inner energy throbbings with *chi yi* breathing.

4. Continue to monitor the throbbings for at least 50 to 100 counts. You should begin to feel relief.

APPLICATION 13

Relieving Motion Sickness

At the first hint of discomfort, do the following:

1. Bring on inner energy throbbings with *chi yi* breathing.

2. Monitor your lower abdominal throbs for at least 10 to 30 seconds.

3. Focus your mind on the most uncomfortable spots in your abdomen, stomach, and throat and activate throbbings in those areas.

4. Continue monitoring these throbbings until you feel relief.

5. Breathe deeply and relax. This application may be repeated as frequently as necessary.

APPLICATION 14

Improving Speech and Singing (Vowel Production)

Each different vowel sound you produce requires a subtle variation in the way you exhale. It is important to realize the connection between such intricate adjustments of exhalation and the flow of inner energy. To some extent those adjustments are made by reflex, without any conscious effort. However, when these sounds are coordinated with selective inner energy support, you can produce each sound with a much higher degree of efficiency, which can help mend a damaged voice or add proficiency to an ordinary voice.

You use one finger to play a note on a piano. It is neither necessary nor effective to use all five fingers at once to play one note. Along this same line of reasoning, you should use your inner energy appropriately and deftly to attain the vocal production of an intended sound and to avoid clumsiness, wasted effort, or even injury.

Figures 87 through 93 show the locations of concentrated inner energy formed for producing various vowels commonly used in English and other European languages. Use these figures as a guide in helping you to direct your inner energy to the appropriate locations.

The following application will help you to achieve increased vocal proficiency. Starting with the vowel "ah" (as in "father"), visualize the image in Figure 87 as you imagine your torso to be a big hollow barrel. (Note that Figures 91 and 93 show the back of the torso.)

1. Inhale deeply to the bottom of the barrel, according to the principles of *chi yi*.

2. Open your mouth wide in preparation for producing a *hah* sound. Be sure your jaws are parted not only in front but all the way back to the jaw hinges so that the top and bottom molars are evenly parted and almost parallel.

3. Exhale with a *hah* sound, as if letting air reverberate in the empty barrel. Simultaneously imagine the shaded area in

Figure 87 as air vent(s) cut out at the front of the barrel. Imagine air ventilating through these cutout(s) as you exhale in a long, sustained, aspirated, whispering *hah*. Repeat this step several times.

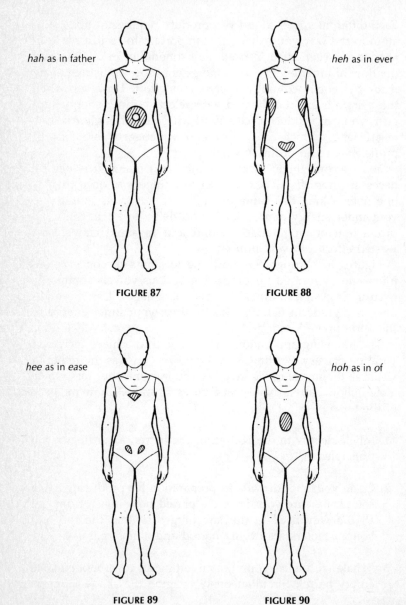

hah as in father

FIGURE 87

heh as in ever

FIGURE 88

hee as in ease

FIGURE 89

hoh as in of

FIGURE 90

4. Repeat steps 1 through 3, but in place of the aspirated, sustained, whispering *hah* substitute a vocal *hah*, as in regular speech. (Singers may substitute the singing of a legato *hah* at a comfortable pitch.)

hu as in would

huh as in her

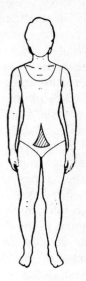

FIGURE 91

FIGURE 92

hü as in French *u* and German *ü;* combination of *ee* and *ou* sounds, with rounded lips

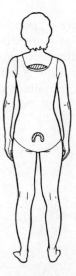

FIGURE 93

Use steps 3 and 4 to practice through all the vowels illustrated in Figures 87 through 93, one vowel at a time, being sure to open your mouth sufficiently. Certain vowels in speech or singing may present you with more difficulty than others, and these problem vowels will cause a scratchy, uncomfortable sensation. If left unattended, the inefficient execution of these vowels in everyday speech will contribute to injury and damage to the vocal cords. Spend more time practicing these problem sounds, being sure to use proper breath support and appropriate mouth and tongue positions. Use the figures as a guide to the distribution of inner energy to improve your placement of vowels and vowel production and to gradually eliminate this vocal difficulty.

As you progress, you will be able to combine various vowels in any sequence to gain further control and versatility in the allocation of inner energy. Try, for instance, to say in one breath *hah—heh—hah—heh—hah—*. As you produce these sounds, train your mind's eye to visualize core energy at the locations shown in Figures 87 and 88, alternating locations as you alternate sounds. In the same manner, you can also try *hah—heh—hee—hoh—hoo—he(r)—hü—* or any other combination that suits your needs. For instance, if you have difficulty in pronouncing or singing the word "into," practice *hee—hoo—hee—hoo—hee—hoo* until this vowel combination is smoothed out.

By selecting a specific vowel to practice, you will isolate a specific area of your torso to develop and strengthen.

Vowels form the backbone of speech and singing; once they have been sturdily constructed, consonants will have a much better chance of falling properly into place.

Simplified Vowel Exercise

The following simplified version of the previous vowel exercise may be used to help stimulate isolated areas of the torso; to emphatically activate the inner energy flow, a section at a time; and to bring on inner energy surges and throbs.

1. Breath deeply, using the principles learned in this book. Review one or more of the following imagery drills: Eyedropper, Sink and Drain, or Coil of Rope.

2. Open your mouth in preparation for producing a whispering aspirated *hah* sound. Be sure your jaws are parted not only in front but all the way to the jaw hinges, so that the top and bottom molars are almost parallel.

3. Relax your tongue and place the tongue tip behind the bottom front teeth. Exhale air sparingly, producing a sustained *hah* sound. Simultaneously visualize Figure 87, imagining that the shaded area is cut out. Imagine air ventilating through this cutout in your torso in a long, sustained, aspirated, whispering *hah* sound. As you do this several times, you will feel a slight warmth in the part of your body corresponding to the shaded area.

Use the above three steps to produce all the vowels illustrated in Figures 87 through 93 in the same whispering aspirated and sustained manner. As you produce each of these sounds, visualize the figure that corresponds to the sound you are producing. Be sure to imagine the air ventilating through the shaded areas in each figure.

All these vowel sounds may also be aspirated consecutively in one breath. For example, you may aspirate *hah—heh—hee—hoh—hu—he(r)—hü*. Or *hah—hoh—hah—hoh*. Or *hoh—hu—he(r)—hoh—hü—huh*.

To get the maximum benefit from this exercise, be sure to accompany each sound with the image of the figure that illustrates it. For example, if you aspirate *hoh* while imagining the air ventilating through the corresponding area at the center of your stomach (see Figure 90), the aspirating of the sound will induce inner energy to that specific area, relieving any discomfort in the stomach. An aspirated *he(r)* will not only benefit the specific area depicted in Figure 92, but will also help anchor the inhalations that follow, drawing the inhaled air to the core.

Afterword

Now that you have completed the exercises, applications of *chi yi* principles, and imagery drills described in this book, you have built a solid, effective deep breathing system to support whatever activities you pursue. You are well on your way to achieving the major objective of *chi yi*—to derive the maximum benefit from every breath you inhale. As you continue to apply the principles of deep breathing to your everyday activities, remember that the more you practice breathing to the core, the more energy is stored and ready for use. By stimulating the core regularly and frequently with proper deep breathing, the compounded energy that you develop will improve both your mental sharpness and your physical performance.

Remember, the more you practice *chi yi*, the more adept you will become, and the easier and more natural the techniques will feel. Motivation, concentration, and persistence will pay off; as *chi yi* becomes habitual, you will gain in stamina, grace, radiance, and well-being.

All of the exercises in this book have been carefully planned to accomplish specific purposes. Now that you have mastered those exercises, you can put together your own program, repeating those exercises that you find especially beneficial and combining them in different sequences. If a particular imagery drill helps you with your *chi yi* breathing, use it frequently until the effect wears off, and then substitute another one—or invent one of your own.

Stay flexible in your approach, experiment sensibly, and adjust these exercises to fit your individual needs. Practice an exercise or two before engaging in your favorite sport, or whenever you feel in need of an energy boost. The investment of a few minutes a day will make an amazing difference in your overall performance.

Above all, it is my sincere hope that you will enjoy not only the actual practice of *chi yi*, but all of the physical and mental benefits it brings as well.

About the Author

Nancy Zi was born in the United States and raised in China. She attended Millikin University in Illinois, where she majored in vocal performance and received a bachelor's degree in music. She has more than twenty years of experience in teaching singing and has performed as a professional vocal soloist in concerts, operas, operettas, oratorios, and on TV and radio programs. With her husband, Paul Li, she divides her time between Hong Kong and California. They have two children.

Influenced by the language, culture, and music of both East and West, Nancy Zi has combined her "addiction" to classical singing with her interest in the ancient Chinese discipline of *chi kung* (breath manipulation) to create a new way to acquire a sound breathing technique, which she calls *chi yi*, the art of breathing. Through the direct approach of teaching *chi yi*, the author hopes to dispel the mysticism that surrounds the ancient art of breath manipulation and generation of inner energy to improve overall performance and well-being. In her book, *The Art of Breathing*, Nancy Zi discusses what she has learned and developed—a program of effective breathing principles accessible to an international audience.